Consonants

★기역 [g], [k]	니은 [n]	디귿 [d], [t]	리을 [r], [l]
ㄱ	ㄴ	ㄷ	ㄹ

지읒 [j], [ch]	치읓 [ch]	키읔 [k]	티읕 [t]
ㅈ	ㅊ	ㅋ	ㅌ

쌍기역 [kk]	쌍디귿 [tt]	쌍비읍 [pp]	쌍시옷 [ss]
ㄲ	ㄸ	ㅃ	ㅆ

Vowels

[a]	[eo]	[o]	[u]
ㅏ	ㅓ	ㅗ	ㅜ

[ya]	[yeo]	[yo]	[yu]
ㅑ	ㅕ	ㅛ	ㅠ

[wa]	[weo]	[wae]	[we]
ㅘ	ㅝ	ㅙ	ㅞ

미음 [m]	비읍 [b], [p]	시옷 [s], [sh]	이응 [ng]
ㅁ	ㅂ	ㅅ	ㅇ

피읖 [p]	히읗 [h]
ㅍ	ㅎ

쌍지읒 [jj]
ㅉ

★The title of each consonant

[eu]	[i]	[ae]	[e]
ㅡ	ㅣ	ㅐ	ㅔ

[yae]	[ye]
ㅒ	ㅖ

[oe]	[wi]	[ui]
ㅚ	ㅟ	ㅢ

2nd edition

Korean made easy · Starter

Korean made easy · Starter `2nd edition`

Written by	Seung-eun Oh
Translated by	Ryan P. Lagace, Isabel Kim Dzitac
Illustrated by	Moon-su Kim, Byung-chul Yoon

First Published	October, 2009
Second Edition	April, 2022
Second Printing	June, 2023
Publisher	Kyu-do Chung
Editor	Suk-hee Lee, Inkyung Park
Designer	Na-kyoung Kim, Ji-young Yoon, Hyun-ju Yoon
Voice Actor	So-yun Shin, Rae-whan Kim, Toosix Media

DARAKWON Published by Darakwon Inc.

Darakwon Bldg., 211 Munbal-ro, Paju-si, Gyeonggi-do
Republic of Korea 10881
Tel : 82-2-736-2031   Fax : 82-2-732-2037
(Marketing Dept. ext.: 250~252, Editorial Dept. ext.: 420~426)

ISBN : 978-89-277-3276-1 14710
       978-89-277-3272-3 (set)

http://www.darakwon.co.kr
http://koreanbooks.darakwon.co.kr

※ Visit the Darakwon homepage to learn about our other publications and promotions,
   and to download the contents in MP3 format.

Korean made easy Starter

2nd edition

Seung-eun Oh

Preface

〈Korean Made Easy〉 시리즈는 제2언어 혹은 외국어로서 한국어를 공부하는 학습자를 위해 집필되었다. 특히 이 책은 시간적·공간적 제약으로 인해 정규 한국어 교육을 받을 수 없었던 학습자를 위해 혼자서도 한국어를 공부할 수 있도록 기획되었다. 〈Korean Made Easy〉 시리즈는 초판 발행 이후 오랜 시간 독자의 사랑과 지지를 받으며 전 세계 다양한 언어로 번역되어 한국어 학습에 길잡이 역할을 했다고 생각한다. 이번에 최신 문화를 반영하여 예문을 깁고 연습 문제를 보완하여 개정판을 출판하게 되어 저자로서 크나큰 보람을 느낀다. 한국어를 공부하려는 모든 학습자가 〈Korean Made Easy〉를 통해 효과적으로 한국어를 공부하면서 즐길 수 있기를 바란다.

시리즈 중 〈Korean Made Easy - Starter (2nd Edition)〉은 한글을 전혀 읽지 못하는 학습자를 위한 입문서이다. 한글은 누구나 몇 시간 안에 쉽게 배울 수 있는 과학적인 언어 체계를 지녔다. 이 책은 그러한 한글의 과학적 체계를 설명할 뿐만 아니라, 듣고 발음하고 읽고 쓰는 다양한 연습 활동과 게임을 통해 즐겁게 한글을 공부할 수 있도록 고안된 책이다. 궁극적으로 학습자가 일상생활에서 자주 접하는 어휘나 표현을 익히도록 설계되었다. 〈Korean Made Easy - Starter (2nd Edition)〉 단 한 권만으로 학습자가 한글을 완벽하게 이해하고 표현할 수 있도록 하는 것이 이 책의 목표이다. 한글을 가르치는 초보 교사가 한글을 어떻게 가르칠지 고민이 될 때에도 이 책이 알차고 즐거운 수업을 준비하는 데 도움이 되기를 기대한다.

〈Korean Made Easy - Starter (2nd Edition)〉은 크게 "한글 소개"와 한글을 배우는 "10개 과", "24개의 중요 표현"으로 나뉘어 있다. "한글 소개"는 본격적으로 한글을 익히기 이전에 영어와 너무 다른 한국어의 특징을 이해할 수 있도록 설명한 것이다. "10개 과"는 각 과가 "준비하기 – 공부하기 – 읽기 활동 – 쓰기 활동 – 종합 문제"의 다섯 단계로 구성되어 있는데, 각 단계에서 다양한 연습 문제와 듣기 자료가 제공되어 학습자가 책의 구성을 따라가는 것만으로도 체계적이고 재미있게 한국어를 학습할 수 있도록 하였다. "24개의 중요 표현"은 한국 생활에서 꼭 알아 두어야 할 표현 24개를 상황 그림과 함께 카드로 제작하여 학습자가 들고 다니면서 적절한 상황에 바로 사용할 수 있도록 하였다.

이 책은 많은 분의 도움으로 완성될 수 있었다. 먼저, 이 책의 초판 원고 내용을 영어로 정확하고 분명하게 번역해 주신 Ryan Lagace 선생님께 감사드린다. 교정 과정에서 영어권 학습자에게 쉽고 유익한 설명이 되도록 조언과 의견을 아낌없이 주신 Elizabeth Barns 씨께도 진심으로 감사드리고 싶다. 자신의 한국어 학습 경험을 바탕으로 "한글 소개"의 내용에 소중한 의견을 주신 Ann Kidder 씨와, 교정 단계에서 자질구레한 실수를 하지 않도록 꼼꼼하게 원고를 읽어 주시고 조언을 아끼지 않았던 James Platte 씨께도 이 자리를 빌려 감사드리고 싶다. 아울러, 이 책의 개정판 번역과 교정 과정을 훌륭하게 해 주신 Isabel Kim Dzitac 씨께도 진심으로 감사의 인사를 드린다. 이분들의 도움이 있었기에 책의 완성도가 한층 높아졌다고 믿는다. 또한 한국어 교육에 많은 애정과 관심을 보여 주시는 다락원의 정규도 사장님과 좋은 책을 만들고자 어려운 길을 마다하지 않는 다락원 한국어출판부의 편집진께도 진심으로 감사의 말씀을 전한다.

마지막으로 저자가 마음 편히 책을 완성할 수 있도록 언제나 곁에서 응원해 주시고 기도해 주시는 어머니, 그리고 하늘에서 이 책을 보고 너무도 기뻐해 주실 아버지께 이 책을 바치고 싶다.

오승은

The *Korean Made Easy* series was written for non-native Korean language learners. In particular, this book was designed for learners who cannot receive regular Korean language education. The *Korean Made Easy* series has been loved and supported by readers for a long time since its first edition. It has since been translated into various languages around the world and has served as a guide to those learning Korean. I feel rewarded as an author, as the revised version offers supplemental exercises that incorporate example sentences reflecting the culture of the present. I hope that all learners who want to study Korean can study Korean effectively and enjoyably through *Korean Made Easy*.

Among the series, *Korean Made Easy - Starter (2nd Edition)* is an introductory book for learners who cannot read any Korean. Hangeul has a scientific language system that anyone can easily learn within a few hours. This book is designed not only to explain the scientific system of Hangeul, but also to make learning Hangeul enjoyable through various practice activities and games centered on listening, pronouncing, reading, and writing. Ultimately, it is created to help familiarize learners with vocabulary or expressions frequently encountered in daily life. The goal of this book, *Korean Made Easy - Starter (2nd Edition)*, is to enable learners to fully understand and express Korean with just one book. I also hope that this book will help instructors, who are concerned about how to teach Hangeul, prepare for a fruitful and enjoyable class.

Korean Made Easy - Starter (2nd Edition) consists of an introduction, ten chapters of lessons, and twenty-four useful expressions. The introduction aims to explain how Korean differs from English and highlight the distinguishing characteristics of the Korean language before learners begin studying Hangeul. Each lesson chapter is divided into five steps that contain plenty of practice exercises and audio components. It is my hope that this systemic structure eases learners in their study of Korean. In addition, twenty-four useful expressions that are necessary to know in everyday life are provided on cards with situational pictures. These cards are designed for learners to use and carry out expressions in appropriate situations or contexts.

This book was made possible thanks to the efforts of many. First, I would like to thank Ryan Lagace for his precise and clear translation of this book into English. I would like to thank Elizabeth Barns for her advice and opinions during the revision process on explanations that would be easier and more useful for learners. I also need to thank Ann Kidder for her valuable opinion of the introduction from a learner's perspective. And thanks to James Platte for catching mistakes during the revision process and for offering advice on how to make this book more approachable for native English-speaking learners. In addition, I would like to express my sincere thanks to Isabel Kim Dzitac, who has done an excellent job of translating and proofreading the revised edition of this book. I truly believe that these individuals have contributed greatly to the quality of this book. I thank Kyu-do Chung, President of Darakwon, who has shown great affection and care about Korean language education. I also give my sincere thanks to the editors of the Korean Editorial Department at Darakwon who spent a great deal of effort in finalizing this book.

Lastly, this book is dedicated to my mother, who showered me with her continual support from day one of this project to its completion, and to my late father, who would be pleased with the outcome.

Seung-eun Oh

How to Use This Book

★ Introduction

The formation of syllables, pronunciation method, and sentence structure of the Korean language are very different from those in English. This part takes a look at those differences and uses illustrations to easily present pertinent information that English speakers should know before beginning to study Korean.

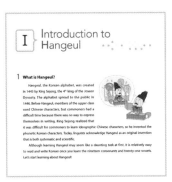

Part 1

Part 1 covers how Korean vowels and consonants are formed, as well as the structure of Korean syllables.

Part 2

Part 2 explains how the structure of Korean syllables is very different from English by showing how Koreans read words that came from English.

Part 3

Part 3 covers the differences between English and Korean sentence structures. It helps learners attain a comprehensive understanding of Korean sentences.

★ Lesson Chapters

This part comprises of ten chapters that cover Korean vowels and consonants. Each chapter is divided into five steps: 'Let's Warm Up!', 'Let's Study!', 'Reading Activity!', 'Writing Activity!', and 'Quiz Yourself!'. An audio clip with various listening exercises accompanies each step and allows learners to become familiar with Korean on their own. Each portion is voiced twice. The answers to the practice exercises can be found in the appendix.

▶ STEP 1 Let's Warm Up!

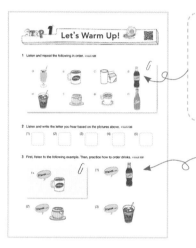

Visual Aids
Through listening exercises, learners can focus their attention on the pronunciation of objects or concepts commonly encountered in everyday life in Korea.

Practice Exercises
This part combines the above-learned objects or concepts with useful Korean expressions. It also allows learners to practice conversations based on pictures rather than text. Learners can become accustomed with Korean expressions by listening to the audio and practicing. The complete listening script can be found in the appendix.

▶ STEP 2 Let's Study!

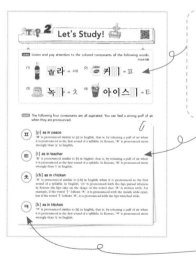

Listen
This part reinforces the pronunciation of objects or concepts in Step 1. The corresponding vowels or consonants are presented as the learning objective of Step 2.

Learn
The pronunciation and explanation of the target vowels or consonants for each chapter are presented with visual aids.

* An in-depth explanation of target vowels or consonants that cause difficulties for English speakers is provided.

Pronunciation Symbols
The pronunciation symbols of target vowels or consonants are romanized. By listening and repeating to the audio, you can become familiar with the pronunciation of Korean vowels or consonants as well as the pronunciation symbols.

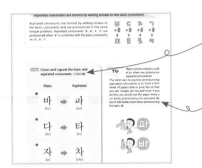

Practice

Each chapter has audio segments to practice the pronunciation of the target vowels or consonants.

Pronunciation Tip

Pronunciation tips are provided for target vowels or consonants that cause difficulty for English speakers.

▶ **STEP 3** **Reading Activity!**

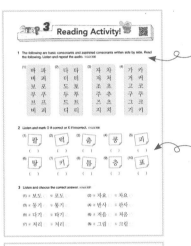

Reading Syllables

This part provides reading practice of previously learned vowels or consonants combined with the target vowels or consonants. Learners can practice their pronunciation by listening to the audio component while following along with the text.

Practice Exercises for Syllables and Words

This part is divided into two parts that provide practice exercises for reading syllables and words. All of the exercises require learners to use the audio component.

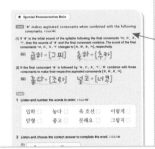

Special Pronunciation Rule

This part provides a simple explanation of the pronunciation rules related to the target vowels or consonants. Learners can become familiar with the pronunciation rules where the pronunciation differs from the spelling by working through practice exercises on the audio component.

▶ **STEP 4** **Writing Activity!**

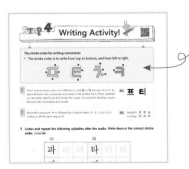

Stroke Order and Tips

This part presents the correct stroke order of the target vowels or consonants as well as tips on how to avoid writing mistakes commonly made by English-speaking learners.

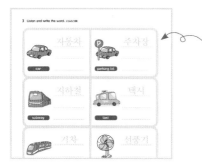

Writing Practice Exercises

This part allows learners to check their pronunciation and spelling by completing various writing exercises on words presented in the reading exercises in Step 3.

▶ **STEP 5** Quiz Yourself!

This part consists of fun games with words that combine the target vowels or consonants and previously learned vowels or consonants offer learners comprehensive practice. With visual aids and various exercises, learners can easily make the connection between the pronunciation and meaning of words. Also, this step presents useful words for real-life situations so that learners can not only practice how to read vowels and consonants but also acquire new vocabulary in a meaningful way.

★ Twenty-four Useful Expression Cards

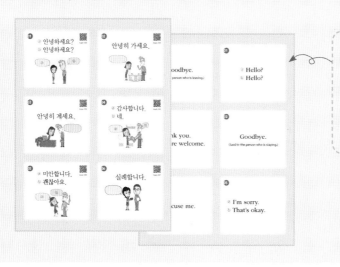

Twenty-four useful expressions are provided on cards that learners can use when they encounter different situations with Koreans. These cards are designed for learners to carry and to use in appropriate situations.

Contents

Table of Contents

★ Introduction

Part	Contents
1	**Introduction to Hangeul:** Short history of Hangeul; Etymology of vowels and consonants; Building syllables;
2	**Characteristics of Korean Vowels and Consonants:** One sound per syllable; Requirement to have a vowel
3	**Characteristics of Korean Sentences:** Location of verbs; Conjugation of verbs and adjectives; Using markers;

★ 10 Lesson Chapters

| Stroke order |
| with each consonant; Dropping of 'r' in pronunciation; Different consonant sounds between Korean and English |
| Matching structure for questions and answers; Using honorific forms; Style of speech |

	Vocabulary in Reading and Writing	Special Pronunciation Rules	Vocabulary Review
	아 (감탄), 아우, 아이, 어이, 오 (다섯), 오이, 이 (둘), 이 (치아)		
	나라, 나리, 나무, 너무, 노루, 누나, 마무리, 머루, 머리, 모이, 무리, 미리, 어머니, 어미, 오리, 우리, 이마, 이모, 이미		
	가수, 거리, 고구마, 고기, 구두, 그리고, 기사, 기자, 다시, 도시, 두부, 드라마, 모두, 모자, 바다, 바로, 바지, 버스, 보기, 비, 서로, 아버지, 오후, 자리, 지도, 지하, 하나, 하루, 허리, 후기		
	가방, 강, 거울, 공항, 국, 남산, 남자, 눈, 다섯, 돈, 문, 미국, 바람, 밥, 부모님, 사랑, 사진, 선물, 수업, 시간, 시작, 아들, 아줌마, 옷, 우산, 운동, 음식, 이름, 일곱, 점심, 젓가락, 정말, 종이, 주말, 집, 한국, 한복	녹음, 단어, 발음, 언어, 얼음, 웃음, 음악, 직업	Directions (동, 서, 남, 북) Natural features (산, 나무, 강, 절, 섬, 하늘, 구름, 비, 바람, 눈)
	경기, 공연, 귤, 금연, 목욕, 무료, 병, 수영, 아니요, 안경, 안녕, 야구, 약, 양말, 양복, 여기, 여자, 역, 연습, 영수증, 영어, 요금, 요리, 요즘, 우유, 유명, 일요일, 저녁, 조용, 학교, 현금, 형	국민, 벚나무, 빗물, 숙녀, 식물, 업무, 입문, 잇몸, 작년	Seasons (봄, 여름, 가을, 겨울)
	가게, 계단, 계산, 계속, 내일, 냄새, 냉장고, 넷, 노래, 매일, 맥주, 문제, 배, 벌레, 베개, 비행기, 색, 생각, 생선, 생일, 선생님, 세계, 소개, 숙제, 시계, 실례, 아내, 아래, 얘기, 어제, 예술, 예약, 오래, 재미, 해	난리, 설날, 신라, 신랑, 실내, 연락, 진료	
	경찰, 경치, 기차, 김치, 남편, 도착, 보통, 부탁, 스포츠, 아침, 연필, 우체국, 자동차, 주차장, 지하철, 책, 처음, 추석, 출구, 출발, 춤, 층, 친구, 친절, 침대, 카메라, 컴퓨터, 크림, 택시, 통역, 포도, 표, 핸드폰	높다, 맏형, 못해요, 비슷해요, 생각해요, 연습해요, 육 호선, 이렇게, 입학, 좋다, 축하, 행복해요	Countries (한국, 미국, 중국, 영국, 일본, 호주, 독일, 인도, 캐나다, 프랑스, 필리핀, 베트남) Famous locations in Seoul (명동, 남산, 시청, 홍대, 남대문 시장, 동대문 시장, 경복궁, 광화문, 강남역, 서울역, 이태원, 종로)
	가위, 과일, 과자, 관심, 교회, 대사관, 더워요, 돼지, 뒤, 매워요, 문화, 뭐, 바퀴, 병원, 분위기, 사과, 쉬워요, 영화, 왜, 외국, 위, 위험, 의사, 전화, 죄송, 주의, 최고, 취미, 취소, 화장실, 회사, 훼손, 휘파람	거의, 무늬, 예의, 의미, 의사, 의자, 주의, 편의점, 회의, 희망, 흰색	Days of the week (월요일, 화요일, 수요일, 목요일, 금요일, 토요일, 일요일) Places (은행, 시장, 주유소, 편의점, 병원, 약국, 영화관, 공원, 교회, 식당, 카페, 화장실, 지하철역, 학교, 공항, 집, 주차장) Jobs (선생님, 학생, 경찰, 회사원, 주부, 가수, 의사, 간호사, 기자, 화가)
	가끔, 기뻐요, 깜짝, 꼭, 꿈, 느낌, 딸, 딸기, 땀, 때문, 떡, 뚜껑, 뜻, 바빠요, 비싸요, 빨래, 빨리, 빵, 싸요, 쌈, 쓰레기통, 씨, 아저씨, 오른쪽, 오빠, 이따가, 잠깐, 찌개, 찜질방	갑자기, 낮잠, 늦게, 듣기, 목소리, 박수, 숟가락, 습관, 식당, 약속, 역시, 옷장, 입구, 책상, 혹시	Fruits (사과, 배, 딸기, 포도, 수박, 바나나, 감, 귤)
	값, 까닭, 꽃, 끝, 닭, 닭고기, 돌솥, 몇, 무릎, 밑, 밖, 부엌, 빛, 삶, 숯불, 숲, 앉아요, 않아요, 여덟, 옆, 있어요, 잎, 흙	많이, 몇 살, 밑줄, 밖, 볶음, 싫어요, 앞, 없어요, 옆집, 잃어요, 젊음	Locations (앞, 뒤, 옆, 오른쪽, 왼쪽, 위, 아래, 안, 밖) Body parts (머리, 눈, 코, 귀, 입, 목, 어깨, 가슴, 배, 팔, 손, 허리, 다리, 무릎, 발)

I Introduction to Hangeul

1 What is Hangeul?

Hangeul, the Korean alphabet, was created in 1443 by King Sejong, the 4ᵗʰ king of the Joseon Dynasty. The alphabet spread to the public in 1446. Before Hangeul, members of the upper class used Chinese characters, but commoners had a difficult time because there was no way to express themselves in writing. King Sejong realized that it was difficult for commoners to learn ideographic Chinese characters, so he invented the phonetic Korean characters. Today, linguists acknowledge Hangeul as an original invention that is both systematic and scientific.

Although learning Hangeul may seem like a daunting task at first, it is relatively easy to read and write Korean once you learn the nineteen consonants and twenty-one vowels. Let's start learning about Hangeul!

2 How was Hangeul formed?

(1) Vowels

There are twenty-one vowels in Hangeul that are formed with 'Cheon (Sky: ●)', 'Ji (Ground: ─)', and 'In (Person: |)'.

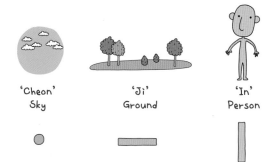

'Cheon'
Sky

'Ji'
Ground

'In'
Person

For example, the vowel 'ㅏ' is formed by writing 'Cheon (●)' to the right of 'In (ㅣ)' and the vowel 'ㅗ' is formed by writing 'Ji (ㅡ)' under 'Cheon (●)'.

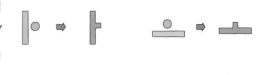

Vowels formed by adding 'Cheon (●)' to 'In (ㅣ)' are called vertical vowels, and those formed by adding 'Cheon (●)' to 'Ji (ㅡ)' are called horizontal vowels. Consonants are placed differently when paired with vertical vowels versus horizontal vowels. It is also possible to combine two vowels to form compound vowels.

(2) Consonants

There are nineteen consonants in Hangeul, and these are formed by mimicking the shape of the tongue or vocal organs. For example, the shape for 'ㅁ' [m] comes from the shape your lips form when pronouncing this consonant. The shape for 'ㄴ' [n] comes from the shape of the tongue as it briefly touches the back of the upper teeth when this consonant is pronounced.

As shown below, 'ㅁ, ㄴ, ㅅ, ㄱ, ㅇ' are the basic consonants.

| [m] | [n] | [s] or [sh] | [k] or [g] | [ng] |

Additional strokes can be added to each of these basic consonants to produce new consonants. These new consonants are pronounced using the same shape of the tongue or vocal organs as the original basic consonant. For example, by adding additional strokes to 'ㅁ' [m], the consonants 'ㅂ' [b], 'ㅍ' [p], and 'ㅃ' [pp] are formed.

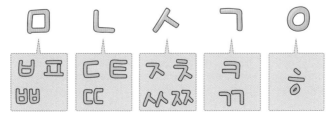

15

3 How are consonants and vowels combined?

In written English, letters with their own unique phonetic sounds are written in a line to produce syllables and words. However, in Korean, consonants and vowels are instead grouped together by syllables like those pictured to the right. If a word has two syllables in Korean, the vowels and consonants for each syllable are grouped together as pictured.

In Korean, each consonant and vowel has its own phonetic sound. However, a consonant must be written with a vowel. Therefore, in Korean, vowels serve as the focus, and consonants are written before or after vowels to form syllables. These are then grouped into words.

In Korean, there are four ways of using syllables by combining vowels and consonants.

❶ **When vowels are used alone (combination of soundless 'o' and vowels)**

In spoken Korean, vowels can produce a sound by themselves. In written Korean, however, the soundless 'o' must be placed in the space before the vowel (the consonant's position). 'o' is written to the left of vertical vowels (ㅏ, ㅓ, ㅣ) and above horizontal vowels (ㅗ, ㅜ, ㅡ).

▸ **Soundless 'o' + Vowels**

| horizontal vowel | vertical vowel | compound vowel |

❷ **When consonants are used before vowels**

The consonant cannot be pronounced alone and can be pronounced with the vowel. The consonant is written in place of the soundless 'o'.

▸ **Initial consonants + Vowels**

| horizontal vowel | vertical vowel | compound vowel |

❸ When consonants are used after vowels

Consonants come after vowels and are called *batchim* (the final consonant of the syllable). As shown, syllables are divided into an upper part and a lower part. *Batchims* are written in the lower part.

▶ Soundless 'o' + Vowels + Final consonants (*batchim*)

horizontal vowel

vertical vowel

compound vowel

❹ When vowels are used between consonants

The first consonant and vowel are written together in the upper part of the syllable, and the second consonant is written in the lower part as the *batchim* (the final consonant of the syllable).

▶ Initial consonants + Vowels + Final consonants (*batchim*)

horizontal vowel

vertical vowel

compound vowel

4 What is the correct stroke order for writing consonants and vowels?

There are two basic rules to follow when writing consonants and vowels. The first is to write from left to right, and the second is to write from top to bottom.

Ⅱ Characteristics of Korean Vowels and Consonants

1 Korean vowels always produce the same sound.

Unlike in English, Korean vowels always produce the same sound. For example, the English vowel 'o' in 'hot' or 'roll' is pronounced differently, but the Korean vowel 'ㅏ' always produces the same sound.

2 Vowels serve as the focus when writing Korean, and consonants are attached before or after vowels.

In English, consonants and vowels are written side by side without separation. In Korean, however, vowels serve as the focus, and consonants are attached before or after vowels. For example, take the word 'camera' written as 카메라 in Korean (three syllables based on three vowels). Each Korean syllable represents in a square like the following.

Ex.　ho-tel 호텔
Ko-re-a 코리아
Ca-na-da 캐나다

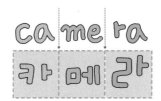

3 In Korean, vowels are required to pronounce consonants.

In English, the word 'bus' is pronounced as one syllable; the final consonant 's' in 'bus' can produce a sound without there being a vowel after it. In Korean, however, the consonant 's' requires the vowel 'ㅡ' to produce a sound, so 'bus' must be written as 버스 (buh-seu) and is pronounced with two syllables. The same applies to the word 'ski', in which the consonants 's' and 'k' produce their own sounds. This is written as 스키 (seu-ki) in Korean, again because the 's' requires the vowel '—' in this word.

Ex.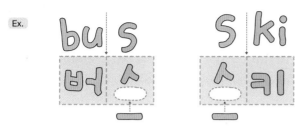

4 Korean basic vowels produce a single, short sound.

In Korean, the basic vowels 'ㅏ'[a], 'ㅗ'[o], and 'ㅐ'[ae] are pronounced without any change in the shape of the lips, which is different from the pronunciation of 'ice'[ai] in English. Multiple syllables (for example, 'ice' becomes 아이스) are necessary to write English one-syllable words like these in Korean.

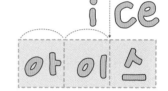

Ex. r<u>i</u>ce 라이스

5 In Korean, the letter 'r' is not pronounced in the middle or end of words.

Korean does not have the English 'r' sound. The 'r' sound is written as 'ㄹ' when it is the initial sound of a word and is not pronounced in the middle or at the end of words. For example, the word 'card' is written as 카 (the consonant 'ㅋ' [k] is attached to the vowel 'ㅏ' [a]) and 드 (the final consonant 'ㄷ' [d] with the vowel '—' [eu]), since there is no sound to pronounce the middle consonant 'r'. So 'card' is written as two syllables 카드 in Korean.

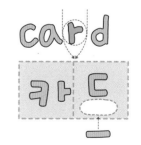

Ex. ma<u>r</u>t 마트 [ma-teu]

car 카 [ka]

6   In Korean, the English consonants 'p/f', 'b/v', and 'l/r' produce the same sound.

In Korean, no distinction is made between the English consonants 'p/f', 'b/v', and 'l/r'. In Korean, 'p/f' are both written as 'ㅍ', 'b/v' as 'ㅂ', and 'l/r' as 'ㄹ'. Therefore, words that have a different meaning in English may be written the same in Korean: pan/fan are both written as 팬, ban/van as 밴, and leader/reader as 리더.

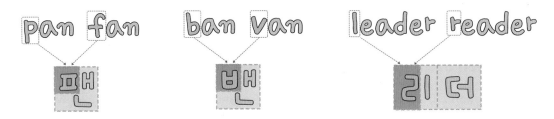

7   There are no sharp 'z' sounds or 'th' sounds in Korean.

In Korean, there are no corresponding sounds like 'z' in pizza or 'th' in 'health'. Thus, the 'z' sound is replaced by 'ㅈ' [j] (ex. pizza → 피자), and the 'th' sound is replaced by 'ㅅ' [s] (ex. health → 헬스).

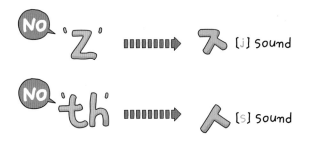

III Characteristics of Korean Sentences

1 The verb is always at the end of the sentence.

As with English, the subject is written in the first part of a Korean sentence. However, unlike English, the verb is always written at the end of the sentence.

Ex. 저는 책을 읽어요.

I read books.

2 In Korean, adjectives can be used at the end of a sentence just like verbs.

In Korean, adjectives can be used as descriptive verbs (to be cheap, to be good, etc.) like English. However, Korean adjectives do not require a verb like 'to be' as they do in English (to be cheap) and can occur alone. They are used at the end of a sentence just like verbs.

Ex. 한국어 단어는 발음하기 쉬워요.

Korean words are easy to pronounce.

3 Korean verbs and adjectives are conjugated by attaching endings to word stems.

The infinitive form of Korean verbs and adjectives is 'stem + 다'. They are conjugated by omitting 다 and attaching various endings. The concept of stems and endings is a characteristic of Korean that is different from English and will take some time to get used to.

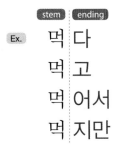

stem	ending
먹	다
먹	고
먹	어서
먹	지만

Ex.

stem	ending
비싸	다
비싸	고
비싸	서
비싸	지만

Ex.

4 Korean uses 'markers'.

In English, the subject and object are discerned by their position in a sentence. However, sentence order cannot be relied on in order to determine the subject and object in Korean, so subject and object markers, as well as time, location, and direction postpositions that act just like English prepositions are used. Since there are markers, as long as the verb is at the very end of the sentence, the order of the subject, object, and other sentence components is not that important. However, sentences generally follow the order of subject, adverb phrase, object, and verb.

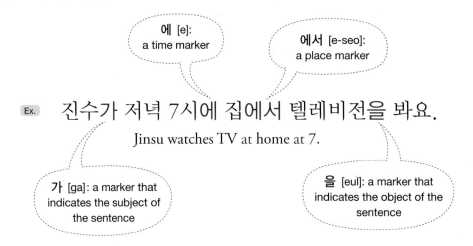

에 [e]: a time marker

에서 [e-seo]: a place marker

Ex. 진수가 저녁 7시에 집에서 텔레비전을 봐요.

Jinsu watches TV at home at 7.

가 [ga]: a marker that indicates the subject of the sentence

을 [eul]: a marker that indicates the object of the sentence

5 The subject is often omitted in Korean.

In colloquial Korean speech, the subject is often omitted. This is especially true for the subject 'I' in first-person declarative sentences and the second-person in questions. Also, when the same subject is repeated in a conversation, it can be dropped after the first mention. Although the subject may be omitted in speech, it is understood from the context.

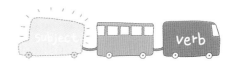

> **Ex.** A: 어디에 가요?   Where are (you) going?
>   (omission of second-person subject)
>
>   B: (저는) 집에 가요. (I) am going home.
>   (omission of first-person subject)

6 In Korean, the sentence order is the same for questions (interrogative sentences) and answers (declarative sentences).

In English, questions (interrogative sentences) are formed by changing the word order. (Example: Who is he? He is Paul.) But, in Korean, the word order does not change when questions are formed. Therefore, in Korean, the sentence order of questions and answers is essentially the same. However, question marks are written at the end of questions, and they end with a rising intonation while periods are written at the end of answers, and they end with a falling intonation. In the case of yes/no questions and wh-questions, the answers have the same structure as the questions.

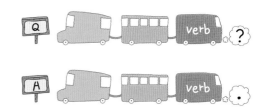

> **Ex.** A: 점심을 먹었어요?   Did you have lunch?
>
>   B: 네, 점심을 먹었어요.   Yes, I had lunch.
>
>   A: 어디에서 먹었어요?   Where did you have (lunch)?
>
>   B: 한식집에서 먹었어요.   I had (lunch) at a Korean-style restaurant.

7 In Korean, the subject and the verb of a sentence do not agree with the person (first-person, second-person, etc.) or singular/plural word.

In English, even when the same verb is used, the form changes according to whether the subject is first-person (I go), third-person (he/she goes), singular (he/she wants), or plural (they want). On the other hand, when the subject changes in Korean, the verb remains the same.

Ex.

제가 학교에 가요.	I go to school.
그 사람이 학교에 가요.	He goes to school.
사람들이 학교에 가요.	People go to school.

8 In Korean, the subject and the verb of a sentence need to agree depending on whether or not honorific forms are used.

In Korean, if the subject of a sentence is someone older or of a higher social status than the speaker, the honorific form must be used. In this case, the verb must have a word ending that denotes the honorific form.

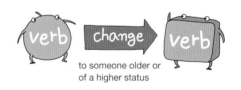

to someone older or of a higher status

Ex.

| (normal) | 친구가 학교에 가요. | My friend goes to school. |
| (honorific) | 아버지가 학교에 가세요. | My father goes to school. |

9 In Korean, different sentence endings are used depending on the conversational setting.

In Korean conversations, different sentence endings are used depending on the setting. –(스)ㅂ니다 is used in formal settings, and –아/어요 is used in informal setting. Sentence endings also change depending on the speaker's relationship to the other party (age, social status, friendliness, etc.).

Ex.

▶ **Depending on the setting**

오늘 날씨가 좋습니다.

The weather is nice today.

(formal setting, for example, a business setting)

오늘 날씨가 좋아요.

The weather is nice today.

(informal setting, for example, a family conversation)

▶ **Depending on the speaker's relationship to the other party**

전화번호를 써 주세요.

Please write your phone number.

(honorific form, for example to your father or mother)

전화번호를 써 줘.

Write your phone number.

(honorific form isn't necessary, for example to your school friends or siblings)

Six Basic Vowels

ㅏ ㅓ ㅗ ㅜ ㅡ ㅣ

Let's Warm Up!

1 Listen and repeat the following in order. ▶ track **001**

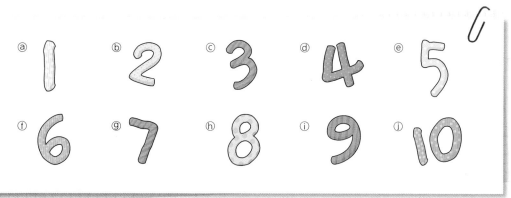

2 Listen and choose the correct answer. ▶ track **002**

(1) 1 ☐ 2 ☐   (2) 3 ☐ 4 ☐   (3) 7 ☐ 8 ☐   (4) 6 ☐ 9 ☐

3 Listen and write the number you hear. ▶ track **003**

(1) ☐   (2) ☐   (3) ☐   (4) ☐

4 Read the following and use the audio to check your answers. ▶ track **004**

(1) 3152 · 3152 ·

(3) 한국무역 홍길동 110-101 서울특별시 종로구 숭월동 141 T.02-736-2031 F.02-732-2036 mobile : 010-9748-6235 e-mail : koera@korea.com

010-9748-6235

외국인등록증 RESIDENCE CARD 981123-495230 NGUYEN CHI VIETNAM 서울특별시 종로구 숭월동 14 서울 출입국 관리사무 종로구출장소장

981123-495230

> **Tip** 0 (zero) is read as [gong], but in this case, [g] has a weak pronunciation. Dash (–) is read as [e].

Listen Read the following. These numbers are written as follows. ▶track **005**

(1) 2 ➡ 이   (2) 5 ➡ 오

Learn The following are the six different basic vowels in Korean. Listen and repeat the audio. ▶track **006**

 [a] as in father
'ㅏ' is pronounced similar to the pronunciation of [a] in English. However, the mouth shouldn't be opened as wide as when [a] is pronounced.

 [eo] as in honest
'ㅓ' is pronounced with the mouth halfway open between [a] and [o]. Keep your jaw still and don't purse your lips. Don't pronounce it strongly.

 [o] as in nobody, *hola* in Spanish
'ㅗ' is pronounced similar to the pronunciation of long [o] in English. However, in Korean 'ㅗ' is pronounced with pursed lips.

 [u] as in who
'ㅜ' is similar to the pronunciation of [u] in English. However, pronounce 'ㅜ' in Korean more briefly compared to [u] in English.

 [eu] as in taken
Pronounce 'ㅡ' with your lips stretched wide like when you smile. Don't pronounce 'ㅡ' strongly. It should be a weak, brief sound.

 [i] as in bee and teeth
Pronounce 'ㅣ' with your lips stretched wide like when you smile. However, the Korean 'ㅣ' is shorter than the sound in teeth.

The soundless 'ㅇ'

In spoken Korean, a vowel can be pronounced as an independent syllable. In writing, however, a vowel cannot stand alone. The soundless 'ㅇ' must be written before the vowel for balance.

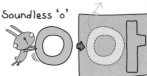

Soundless 'ㅇ'   Consonant Position

For completing the letter

Pronunciation Tip The pronunciation of vowels differs according to how wide the mouth is open, the position of the tongue, and the shape of the lips. Refer to the positions of the lips, as pictured, and use a mirror to make sure that your lips are in similar positions when you pronounce the vowels.

● With the mouth wide open

아

어

● With the lips rounded

오

우

● With the lips stretched wide

으

이

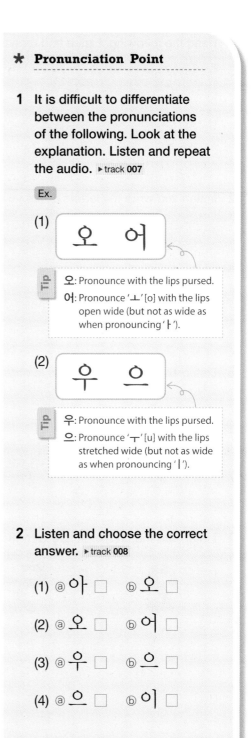

✱ Pronunciation Point

1 It is difficult to differentiate between the pronunciations of the following. Look at the explanation. Listen and repeat the audio. ▶ track **007**

Ex.

(1)

| 오 어 |

Tip 오: Pronounce with the lips pursed.
어: Pronounce 'ㅗ' [o] with the lips open wide (but not as wide as when pronouncing 'ㅏ').

(2)

| 우 으 |

Tip 우: Pronounce with the lips pursed.
으: Pronounce 'ㅜ' [u] with the lips stretched wide (but not as wide as when pronouncing 'ㅣ').

2 Listen and choose the correct answer. ▶ track **008**

(1) ⓐ 아 ☐   ⓑ 오 ☐

(2) ⓐ 오 ☐   ⓑ 어 ☐

(3) ⓐ 우 ☐   ⓑ 으 ☐

(4) ⓐ 으 ☐   ⓑ 이 ☐

1 Read the following. Listen and repeat the audio. ▶ track **009**

ⓐ 아　ⓑ 어　ⓒ 오　ⓓ 우　ⓔ 으　ⓕ 이

2 Listen and write the letters of the vowels you hear above. ▶ track **010**

(1) ⓑ → □ → □ → □ → □ → □

(2) □ → □ → □ → □ → □ → □

3 Listen and number the words in order. ▶ track **011**

아 □　　　이 □　　　아이 □　　　아우 □

오 1　　　어이 □　　　오이 □　　　우이 □

4 Listen and match the picture with the word. ▶ track **012**

(1) 　(2) 　(3) 　(4)

ⓐ 오　　　ⓑ 아이　　　ⓒ 이　　　ⓓ 오이

Writing Activity!

The stroke order for writing vowels

▸ The stroke order of Korean is to write from top to bottom, and from left to right. A circle is drawn counterclockwise starting at the top.

1 Listen and repeat the following syllables after the audio. Write them in the correct stroke order. ▸track **013**

Tip

- When writing the vowels 'ㅏ, ㅓ, ㅗ, ㅜ', the strokes must be joined.

  However, when the soundless 'ㅇ' is written before 'ㅓ, ㅗ', it can be written with or without a space between the circle and the next stroke. Differences can be found in both print and cursive forms, but they indicate the same strokes.

  Ex.1 어 = 어

  Ex.2 오 = 오

- There are times when 'ㅣ' is written as 'ㅣ' or 'ㅇ' is written as 'ㅇ'. This is cursive style and indicates the same stroke.

  Ex.3 이 = 이

2 Listen and complete the word. ▸track **014**

(1)

(2)

(3)

(4)

(5)

(6)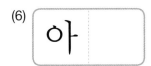

(7)

(8)

3 Listen and write the word. ▸track **015**

이
two

오
five

아이
child

오이
cucumber

이
teeth

아
ah

아우
younger brother

우이
Ui (a place)

 **Quiz Yourself!**

1 Listen and mark O if correct or X if incorrect. ▶ track **016**

(1)
( )

(2)
( )

(3)
( )

(4)
( )

2 Listen and number the words in order. ▶ track **017**

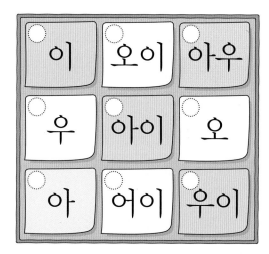

3 Listen and complete the word. ▶ track **018**

(1)

(2)

(3)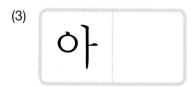

(4)

2

Three Basic Consonants

ㅁ ㄴ ㄹ

Let's Warm Up!

1 Listen and repeat the following in order. ▶track 019

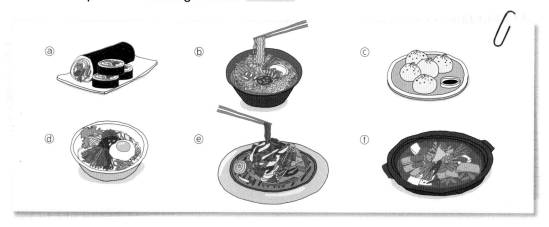

2 Listen and write the letter you hear based on the pictures above. ▶track 020

(1) ⬜   (2) ⬜   (3) ⬜   (4) ⬜   (5) ⬜

3 First, listen to the following examples. Then, listen to the questions on the audio and answer them correctly. ▶track 021

(1)

(2)

(3)

(4)

Listen Listen and pay attention to the initial sound of the first syllable of the following words. ▸ track 022

(1)

(2)

(3)

[m] ➡ ㅁ

[n] ➡ ㄴ

[r] or [ℓ] ➡ ㄹ

Learn The following are the three basic consonants in Korean.

ㅁ

[m] as in money and moon
Similar to the sound of [m] in English.

ㄴ

[n] as in no and now
Similar to the sound of [n] in English.

ㄹ

[r] as in X-ray or [ℓ] as in lollipop
When 'ㄹ' is the first or final sound of a syllable, it is pronounced similar to [ℓ] in English. However, when 'ㄹ' follows a vowel, the tip of the tongue briefly taps the roof of the mouth just behind the teeth, and the pronunciation changes. This sound is written as [r], but it is not pronounced like the English [r], which is pronounced with the tongue flexed toward the back of the mouth.

Practice A vowel is attached after each consonant in order to produce the consonant's sound. Listen and repeat the audio. ▸track **023**

● With a consonant before the vowel 'ㅏ'

❶

아
[a] → 마 [ma]

❷

아
[a] → 나 [na]

❸

아
[a] → 라 [ra]

● With a consonant before the vowel 'ㅗ'

❹

오
[o] → 모 [mo]

❺

오
[o] → 노 [no]

❻

오
[o] → 로 [ro]

● With a consonant before the vowel 'ㅣ'

❼

이
[i] → 미 [mi]

❽

이
[i] → 니 [ni]

❾

이
[i] → 리 [ri]

✱ **Pronunciation Point**

Listen and note how the pronunciation of the consonant 'ㄹ' is different depending on its location.

▸track **024**

Ex.

(1) 라라

(2) 루루

(3) 리리

Reading Activity!

1 Read the following. Listen and repeat the audio. ▶track 025

(1)
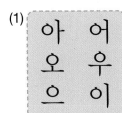
아	어
오	우
으	이

(2)
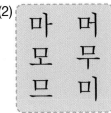
마	머
모	무
므	미

(3)
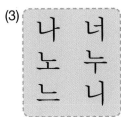
나	너
노	누
느	니

(4)

라	러
로	루
르	리

2 Listen and mark O if correct or X if incorrect. ▶track 026

(1)

머
( )

(2)

노
( )

(3)

리
( )

(4)
무
( )

3 Listen and choose the correct answer. ▶track 027

(1) ⓐ 니 ☐ ⓑ 리 ☐   (2) ⓐ 너 ☐ ⓑ 머 ☐   (3) ⓐ 느 ☐ ⓑ 누 ☐

(4) ⓐ 므 ☐ ⓑ 무 ☐   (5) ⓐ 너 ☐ ⓑ 노 ☐   (6) ⓐ 머 ☐ ⓑ 모 ☐

4 Listen and number the syllables in order. ▶track 028

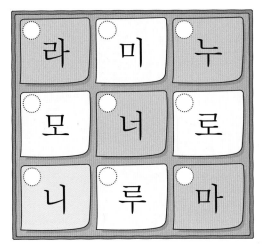

라	미	누
모	너	로
니	루	마

5 Listen and number the words in order. ▶track 029

이미 ☐	이마 ☐	나라 ☐	누나 ☐
어미 ☐	머리 ☐	모이 ☐	머루 ☐
나무 ☐	너무 ☐	우리 ☐	노루 ☐

6 Listen and choose the correct answer to complete the word. ▶track 030

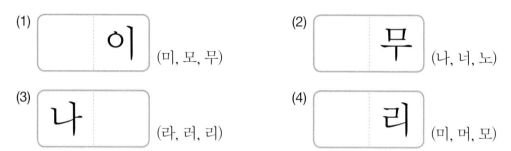

(1) 이 (미, 모, 무)

(2) 무 (나, 너, 노)

(3) 나 (라, 러, 리)

(4) 리 (미, 머, 모)

7 Listen and match the picture with the word. ▶track 031

(1) •

ⓐ 이마

(2) •

ⓑ 나무

(3) •

ⓒ 머리

(4) •

ⓓ 어머니

 **Writing Activity!**

The stroke order for consonants

▸ The stroke order is to write from top to bottom, and from left to right.

• Make sure all four corners are closed so that 'ㅁ' is a closed square.   Ex.1

• When writing 'ㄴ, ㄹ', make sure that none of the strokes overlaps.   Ex.2

1 Listen and repeat the following syllables after the audio. Write them in the correct stroke order. ▸ track **032**

(1)			(2)			(3)		
마	마	마	나	나	나	라	라	라
머	머	머	너	너	너	러	러	러
모	모	모	노	노	노	로	로	로
무	무	무	누	누	누	루	루	루
므	므	므	느	느	느	르	르	르
미	미	미	니	니	니	리	리	리

2 Listen and complete the word. ▶track 033

(1)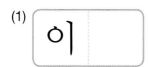

(2)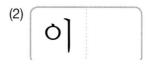

(3)

(4)

(5)

(6)

(7)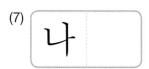

(8) 무

3 Listen and choose the incorrect syllable. Fix the syllable. ▶track 034

Ex. 나 이
① ②
→ 누

(1) 오 리
① ②
→

(2) 이 미
① ②
→

(3) 나 무
① ②
→

(4) 무 리
① ②
→

(5) 나 리
① ②
→

4 Listen and write the word. ▶ track **035**

나이

age

나무

tree

이마

forehead

오리

duck

어머니

mother

머리

head

누나

(male's) elder sister

나라

country

Quiz Yourself!

Listen and follow the path of the words you hear. ▶ track 036

3

Six Basic Consonants

ㅂ ㄷ ㅅ ㅈ ㄱ ㅎ

1 Listen and repeat the following in order. ▶track **037**

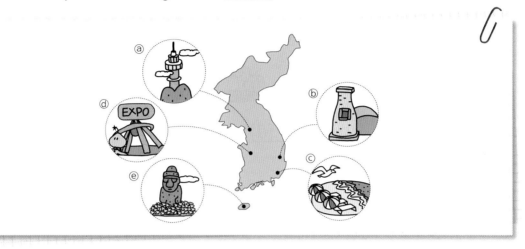

2 Listen and write the letter you hear based on the picture above. ▶track **038**

(1) 　(2) 　(3) 　(4) 　(5)

3 First, listen to the following example. Then, listen to the questions on the audio and answer them correctly. ▶track **039**

 **Let's Study!**

Listen Listen and pay attention to the initial sound of the first syllable of the following words. ▸track **040**

(1)

[b] ➡ ㅂ

(2)

[d] ➡ ㄷ

(3)

[j] ➡ ㅈ

(4)

[g] ➡ ㄱ

(5)

[s] ➡ ㅅ

(6)

[h] ➡ ㅎ

Learn The following are six different consonants in Korean.
Some of these are pronounced in the same position as when pronouncing the consonants studied in Chapter 2 (ㅁ, ㄴ, ㄹ). Some of these new consonants are written by adding strokes to the consonants already learned.

ㅂ [b] **as in table or** [p] **as in pop**
When this consonant is the first or last sound of a syllable, it is pronounced similarly to a weak [p], like when 'p' is pronounced at the end of a word in English. However, when 'ㅂ' is written after a vowel, it is pronounced similarly to the weak [b] sound like the English 'b' when it is pronounced in the middle of a word.

ㄷ [d] **as in studio or** [t] **as in bet**
When this consonant is the first or last sound of a syllable, it is pronounced similarly to a weak [t], like when 't' is pronounced at the end of a word in English. However, when 'ㄷ' is written after a vowel, it is pronounced similar to a weak [d] sound like the English 'd' when it is pronounced in the middle of a word.

[s] as in sky or [sh] as in she

'ㅅ' is pronounced similar to the weak [s] sound in English words that have 's' followed by a consonant. But when 'ㅅ' appears before the vowel ' ㅣ ', the pronunciation becomes similar to that of [sh] in English. Since 'ㅅ' has a weak pronunciation, it is not pronounced as strongly as the 's' in sky.

[j] as in juice or [ch] as in church

When this consonant is the first or last sound of a syllable, it is pronounced similarly to a weak [ch], like when 'ch' is pronounced at the end of a word in English. However, when 'ㅈ' is written after a vowel, it is pronounced similar to a weak [j] sound like the English 'j' when it is pronounced in the beginning of a word.

[g] as in baggage or [k] as in pick

When this consonant is the first or last sound of a syllable, it is pronounced similarly to a weak [k], like when 'k' is pronounced at the end of a word in English. However, when 'ㄱ' is written after a vowel, it is pronounced similar to a weak [g] sound like the English 'g' when it is pronounced in the middle of a word.

[h] as in him

'ㅎ' is pronounced similar to [h] in English.

Consonants cannot be written or pronounced alone

In Korean pronunciation, vowels can stand alone as syllables, but consonants cannot. You cannot begin a syllable with two consonants together (ex. ski, travel), and it must always be combined with a vowel. For example, consider the pronunciation of 'drive' in English and think about how the pronunciation of the two consonants 'd' and 'r' overlap. In order to write this word in Korean, the vowel '—' must be written with the consonant 'ㄷ' [d] and pronounced as 드 [deu] since 'ㄷ' can neither be written nor pronounced independently. In order to complete a syllable, a vowel must always be written with a consonant.

Practice A vowel is attached after each consonant in order to produce the consonant's sound. Listen and repeat the audio. ▶track 041

❶

[a] → [ba]

❷
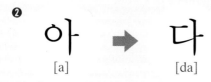
[a] → [da]

❸

[a] → [sa]

❹

[a] → [ja]

❺

[a] → [ga]

❻

[a] → [ha]

Pronunciation **Tip** The sound of the consonants [ㅂ, ㄷ, ㅈ, ㄱ] can change a little depending on their locations.

As the initial sound of a syllable, they are pronounced more similarly to a weak [p, t, ch, k] in English. However, when 'ㅂ, ㄷ, ㅈ, ㄱ' are written after a vowel, they are pronounced similar to the weak [b, d, j, g] in English.

weak [p] as the initial sound of a syllable   [b] following a vowel

* **Pronunciation Point**

1 The consonant of the same syllable changes pronunciation depending on its location. Listen and repeat the audio. ▶track 042

Ex.
(1) 부부 (2) 도도
(3) 주주 (4) 기기

2 The pronunciation of 'ㅅ' changes according to which vowels follow. Listen and repeat the audio. ▶track 043

Ex. 사시 [sashi]
     스시 [seushi]

Tip The pronunciation of 'ㅅ' changes depending on which vowel comes after it.

시: 'ㅅ' is pronounced as [sh] when 'ㅅ' is followed by the vowel 'ㅣ'.

사, 서, 소, 수, 스: 'ㅅ' is pronounced as [s] when 'ㅅ' is followed by 'ㅏ, ㅓ, ㅗ, ㅜ, ㅡ' except the vowel 'ㅣ'.

Reading Activity!

1 Read the following. Listen and repeat the audio. ▶ track 044

(1)
바 버
보 부
브 비

(2)
다 더
도 두
드 디

(3)
사 서
소 수
스 시

(4)
자 저
조 주
즈 지

(5)
가 거
고 구
그 기

(6)
하 허
호 후
흐 히

 When it is followed by a horizontal vowel (ㅗ, ㅜ, ㅡ, etc.), it is written as 'ㄱ' (writing the vertical part of the stroke almost straight down), and when the consonant 'ㄱ' is followed by a vertical vowel (ㅏ, ㅓ, ㅣ, etc.), it is written as 'ㄱ' (curving the vertical part of the stroke to the left).

Ex. (straight) 고 구 그 (curving) 가 거 기

2 Listen and mark O if correct or X if incorrect. ▶ track 045

(1)
( )

(2)
( )

(3)
( )

(4)
( )

(5)
( )

(6)
( )

(7)
( )

(8)
( )

(9)
( )

(10)
( )

3 Listen and choose the correct answer. ▶ track 046

(1) ⓐ 거 □ ⓑ 저 □   (2) ⓐ 니 □ ⓑ 디 □   (3) ⓐ 수 □ ⓑ 주 □

(4) ⓐ 마 □ ⓑ 바 □   (5) ⓐ 더 □ ⓑ 도 □   (6) ⓐ 그 □ ⓑ 구 □

(7) ⓐ 버 □ ⓑ 보 □   (8) ⓐ 수 □ ⓑ 시 □   (9) ⓐ 허 □ ⓑ 호 □

4 Listen and number the words in order. ▶ track 047

바지 □   기자 □   지하 □   드라마 □

가로 □   두부 □   고사 □   아버지 □

무시 □   후기 □   자비 □   도자기 □

5 Listen and choose the correct answer to complete the word. ▶ track 048

(1) 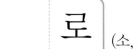 로 (소, 서, 수)

(2) 사  리 (다, 더, 도)

(3) 모  (도, 두, 드)

(4) 고 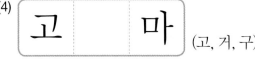 마 (고, 거, 구)

(5)  스 (바, 버, 비)

(6) 나 머  (자, 저, 지)

(7) 다  (사, 서, 시)

(8) 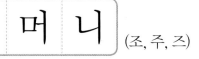 머 니 (조, 주, 즈)

(9) 오  (호, 허, 후)

(10)  무 지 (다, 더, 도)

6 Listen and match the picture with the word. ▶track **049**

(1)  • ⓐ 바지

(2)  • ⓑ 구두

(3)  • ⓒ 모자

(4)  • ⓓ 아버지

7 Listen and number the words in order. ▶track **050**

거리	허리	바다	사자
바로	구이	기사	우주
하나	자리	지하	오후
조사	도시	가수	모기

Writing Activity!

The stroke order for writing consonants

▸ The stroke order is to write from top to bottom, and from left to right.

 Tip The consonants 'ㅅ, ㅈ, ㅎ' look different according to their calligraphic style.   Ex. 시 시 시 지 지 지 히 히 히

 Tip Depending on the calligraphic style, there may be times when it is difficult to read 거, 구, and 그 because they are written without any space between 'ㄱ' and the following vowel. Since every syllable in Korean must have a vowel, if you first locate the vowel, it will be easier to read syllable that may at first appear difficult. Let's practice leaving a space between the consonants and vowels in writing.

Ex.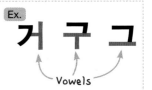

1 Listen and repeat the following syllables after the audio. Write them in the correct stroke order. ▸ track **051**

(1)			(2)			(3)		
바	바	바	다	다	다	사	사	사
버	버	버	더	더	더	서	서	서
보	보	보	도	도	도	소	소	소
부	부	부	두	두	두	수	수	수
브	브	브	드	드	드	스	스	스
비	비	비	디	디	디	시	시	시

	(4)			(5)			(6)		
	자	자	자	가	가	가	하	하	하
	저	저	저	거	거	거	허	허	허
	조	조	조	고	고	고	호	호	호
	주	주	주	구	구	구	후	후	후
	즈	즈	즈	그	그	그	흐	흐	흐
	지	지	지	기	기	기	히	히	히

2 Listen and complete the word. ▶track **052**

(1)
지

(2)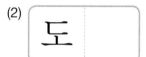
도

(3)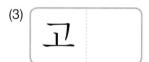
고

(4)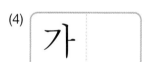
가

(5)
부

(6)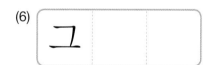
그

(7)
기

(8)
아

(9)
루

(10)
서

3 Listen and write the word. ▶ track 053

비

rain

모자

cap

바지

pants

구두

shoes

지도

map

바다

sea

가수

singer

사자

lion

Quiz Yourself!

1 Listen and choose the correct answer. ▶track 054

(1) ⓐ 조리 ☐   ⓑ 저리 ☐   (2) ⓐ 바지 ☐   ⓑ 비자 ☐

(3) ⓐ 고리 ☐   ⓑ 거리 ☐   (4) ⓐ 조사 ☐   ⓑ 주사 ☐

(5) ⓐ 수다 ☐   ⓑ 다수 ☐   (6) ⓐ 나리 ☐   ⓑ 다리 ☐

(7) ⓐ 서기 ☐   ⓑ 사기 ☐   (8) ⓐ 소수 ☐   ⓑ 조수 ☐

2 Listen and follow the path of the words you hear. Write the word you arrive at.

▶track 055

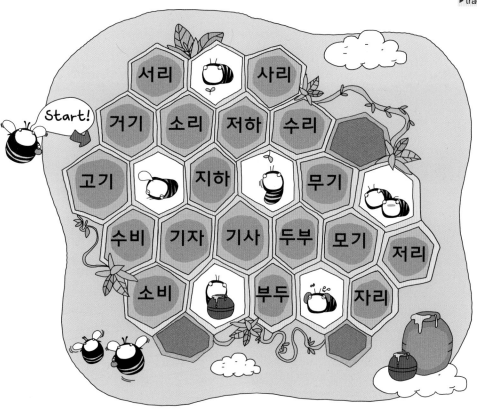

Final Answer: _____

4

Final Consonants

ㅁ ㄴ ㄹ ㅇ
ㅂ ㄷ ㅅ ㅈ ㄱ ㅎ

Let's Warm Up!

1 Listen and repeat the following in order. ▶track **056**

2 Listen and write the letter you hear based on the picture above. ▶track **057**

(1) ☐ (2) ☐ (3) ☐ (4) ☐ (5) ☐ (6) ☐

3 First, listen to the following example. Then, listen to the questions on the audio and answer them correctly. ▶track **058**

Let's Study!

Listen Listen and pay attention to the final sound of the following words. Choose the correct consonant and write it in the space to complete the word. ▶ track **059**

ㄱ   ㅁ   ㄹ   ㅂ

(1)  (2) (3)  (4)

Learn The following consonants are used as *batchims* (the final consonant of the syllable). The consonants written as initial sounds can maintain their phonetic values when written as a final consonant. However, when the soundless 'ㅇ' comes at the end of a syllable, it has the sound [ng]. The air flow abruptly cuts off to pronounce the final consonants more quickly.

ㅁ [m] as in him   ㅂ [p] as in chop

ㄴ [n] as in moon   ㄱ [k] as in book

ㅇ [ng] as in song   ㄷ   [t]
                                                    as in god
ㄹ [ℓ] as in little   ㅈ   [t]

The *batchims* produce seven different sounds

Although all *batchims* can be written, only seven sounds are actually produced. Among the ten letters written below, four of them are pronounced the same when they occur as *batchims*.

ㅁ	ㄴ	ㄹ	ㅇ	ㅂ	ㄱ	ㄷ, ㅅ, ㅈ, ㅎ
[m]	[n]	[ℓ]	[ng]	[p]	[k]	[t]

Practice The *batchim* is written under a vowel. Listen to the following examples and note the difference. ▶ track **060**

❶ When a consonant is the first sound of a syllable

아 ➡ 마
[a]　　　[ma]

❷ When a consonant is the final sound of a syllable (*batchim*)

아 ➡ 암
[a]　　　[am]

Pronunciation Tip When producing the sound of a *batchim*, in order to avoid pronouncing a syllable with a *batchim* as two syllables, be sure to pronounce the vowel quickly.

Ex.

Practice Let's pronounce a *batchim* written under a vowel. Listen and repeat the audio. ▶ track **061**

❶
아 ➡ 암
[a]　　　[am]

❷
아 ➡ 안
[a]　　　[an]

❸
아 ➡ 알
[a]　　　[al]

❹
아 ➡ 앙
[a]　　　[ang]

✱ Pronunciation Point

1 Let's distinguish the pronunciations of the *batchims* '口, ㄴ, ㅇ'. ▶ track **062**

Ex. (1) 삼 : 산 : 상
(2) 감 : 간 : 강
(3) 밤 : 반 : 방
(4) 담 : 단 : 당
(5) 잠 : 잔 : 장
(6) 맘 : 만 : 망

❺

아 → 압

[a] → [ap]

❻

아 → 악

[a] → [ak]

❼

아 → 앋

[a] → [at]

❽

아 → 앗

[a] → [at]

❾

아 → 앚

[a] → [at]

❿

아 → 앟

[a] → [at]

> **Tip**
>
> Don't read 앗 as [a-s] or 앚 as [a-z]. *Batchim* is pronounced shortly and quickly as one syllable.
>
> **Ex.** 앋 = 앗 = 앚 = 앟

---

2 The *batchims* 'ㄷ, ㅅ, ㅈ, ㅎ' are pronounced with the same sound. ▶ track 063

Ex.

(1) 맏 = 맛 = 맞 = 맣
(2) 낟 = 낫 = 낮 = 낳

3 Let's distinguish the pronunciation of the *batchim* 'ㄱ' [k] from the pronunciations of the *batchims* 'ㄷ, ㅅ, ㅈ' [t]. ▶ track 064

Ex. (1) 곡 : 곧
(2) 목 : 못
(3) 낙 : 낮

4 When the final consonant 'ㅎ' is followed by a vowel, 'ㅎ' becomes silent. ▶ track 065

Ex. (1) 좋아요 [조아요]
(2) 놓아요 [노아요]
(3) 넣어요 [너어요]

 **Reading Activity!**

1 Read the following. Listen and repeat the audio. ▶track **066**

(1)
암	엄
옴	움
음	임

(2)
간	건
곤	군
근	긴

(3)
날	널
놀	눌
늘	닐

(4)
상	성
송	숭
승	싱

(5)
압	업
옵	웁
읍	입

(6)
닥	덕
독	둑
득	딕

(7)
안	언
옷	웃
웇	잇

(8)
갇	걷
곳	굿
긎	깅

2 Listen and mark O if correct or X if incorrect. ▶track **067**

(1) 강 ( )　(2) 난 ( )　(3) 돌 ( )　(4) 만 ( )　(5) 국 ( )

(6) 빗 ( )　(7) 낮 ( )　(8) 집 ( )　(9) 곳 ( )　(10) 밥 ( )

3 Listen and choose the correct answer. ▶track **068**

(1) ⓐ공 ☐ ⓑ곰 ☐   (2) ⓐ근 ☐ ⓑ금 ☐   (3) ⓐ장 ☐ ⓑ잔 ☐

(4) ⓐ성 ☐ ⓑ선 ☐   (5) ⓐ목 ☐ ⓑ못 ☐   (6) ⓐ옥 ☐ ⓑ옷 ☐

(7) ⓐ몽 ☐ ⓑ몸 ☐   (8) ⓐ돈 ☐ ⓑ동 ☐   (9) ⓐ북 ☐ ⓑ붓 ☐

4 Listen and number the words in order. ▶ track 069

아들 ☐	도장 ☐	이름 ☐	아줌마 ☐
한국 ☐	음식 ☐	거울 ☐	밀가루 ☐
시간 ☐	남산 ☐	수업 ☐	젓가락 ☐

5 Listen and choose the correct answer to complete the word. ▶ track 070

(1) 바 ☐ (럼, 람, 롬)

(2) 미 ☐ (곡, 격, 국)

(3) 사 ☐ (진, 짐, 징)

(4) 일 ☐ (곱, 곳, 곡)

(5) 소 (잔, 잠, 장)

(6) 다 (섭, 섯, 석)

6 Listen and match the picture with the word. ▶ track 071

(1) (2) (3) Weekend / Mon Tue Wen Thu Fri Sat Sun / 7 8 9 10 11 12 13 (4)

ⓐ 가방　　　ⓑ 버섯　　　ⓒ 주말　　　ⓓ 사진

7 Listen and choose the correct answer. ▶ track 072

(1) ⓐ 정문 ☐　ⓑ 전문 ☐　　(2) ⓐ 정말 ☐　ⓑ 전말 ☐

(3) ⓐ 방문 ☐　ⓑ 반문 ☐　　(4) ⓐ 정기 ☐　ⓑ 전기 ☐

(5) ⓐ 성공 ☐　ⓑ 선공 ☐　　(6) ⓐ 성물 ☐　ⓑ 선물 ☐

★ **Special Pronunciation Rule**

A *batchim* is followed by a vowel.

Learn

In speaking, when a *batchim* is followed by a vowel in the next syllable, the *batchim* is pronounced as the initial sound of the next syllable.

However, when the *batchim* 'ㅇ' is followed by a vowel in the next syllable, the pronunciation is not linked. It keeps its original sound. ▶ track 073

Practice

1 Listen and number the words in order. ▶ track 074

발음 ☐	얼음 ☐	웃음 ☐	녹음 ☐
만일 ☐	단어 ☐	언어 ☐	본인 ☐
직업 ☐	믿음 ☐	금일 ☐	길이 ☐

2 Listen and choose the correct answer to complete the word. ▶ track 075

(1)  음 (발, 밥, 밤)

(2)  웃 (금, 음, 슴)

(3)  어 (단, 담, 당)

(4)  직 (겁, 업, 덥)

(5) 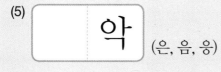 악 (은, 음, 응)

(6)  얼 (음, 름, 릅)

(7)  이 (존, 좀, 종)

(8)  성 (긴, 인, 신)

Writing Activity!

Where to write a *batchim*

▸ Since a *batchim* is the final sound of a syllable, it is written at the bottom (within the same square).

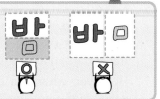

 A syllable with a *batchim* can be difficult to read when the vowel and *batchim* are connected. These syllables can be easier to read if you find the vowel first and then separate the initial and final consonants.

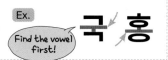

1 Listen and repeat the following syllables after the audio. Write them in the correct stroke order. ▸ track 076

(1)			(2)			(3)		
밤	밤	밤	담	담	담	곤	곤	곤
반	반	반	단	단	단	곳	곳	곳
발	발	발	달	달	달	곶	곶	곶
방	방	방	당	당	당	낫	낫	낫
밥	밥	밥	답	답	답	낮	낮	낮
박	박	박	닥	닥	닥	낳	낳	낳

2 Listen and complete the word. ▸ track 077

(1)

(2)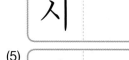

(3)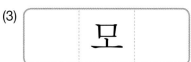

(4)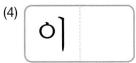

(5)

(6)

3 Listen and write the word. ▶track **078**

집

house

문

door

발

foot

목

neck

돈

money

눈

snow

운동

exercise

공항

airport

음식

food

점심

lunch

한복

Korean traditional dress

옷

clothes

우산

umbrella

선물

present

남자

man

가방

bag

 **Quiz Yourself!**

1 Listen and choose the correct answer. ▶ track 079

(1)
　ⓐ 삼 ☐　　ⓑ 섬 ☐

　ⓒ 솜 ☐　　ⓓ 숨 ☐

(2)
　ⓐ 반 ☐　　ⓑ 번 ☐

　ⓒ 본 ☐　　ⓓ 분 ☐

(3)
　ⓐ 성 ☐　　ⓑ 선 ☐

　ⓒ 섬 ☐　　ⓓ 설 ☐

(4)
　ⓐ 공 ☐　　ⓑ 곤 ☐

　ⓒ 곰 ☐　　ⓓ 골 ☐

2 Listen and number the words in order. ▶ track 080

직업	곧	바람
혼자	멍	빛
동물	장난	식당

3 Listen and complete the word. ▶ track 081

(1) 　　ㄱ | ㅂ

(2) 　　ㅁ | ㄷ

(3) 　　ㅅ | ㅇ

(4) 　　ㅂ | ㅅ

4 Listen and choose the correct answer. ▶ track 082

5 Listen and write the word. ▶track **083**

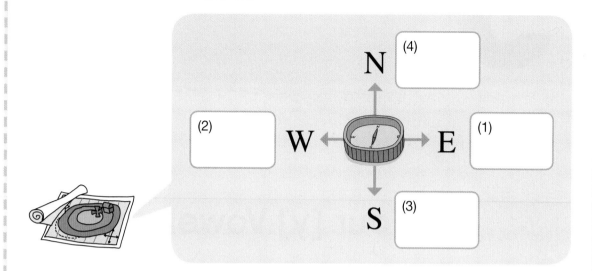

6 Listen and complete the word. ▶track **084**

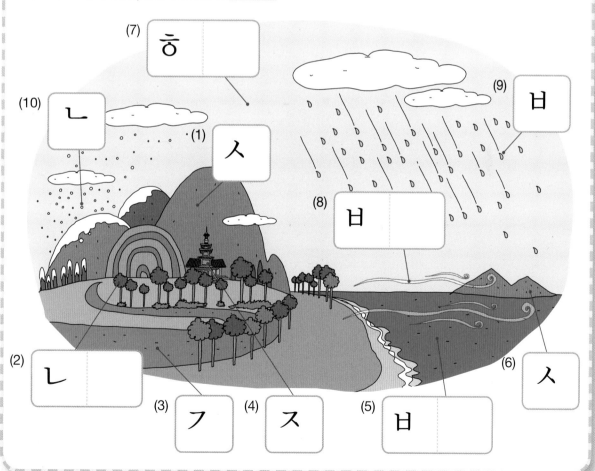

Four [y] Vowels

ㅑ ㅕ ㅛ ㅠ

Let's Warm Up!

1 Listen and repeat the following in order. ▶ track **085**

2 Listen and write the letter you hear based on the pictures above. ▶ track **086**

(1)   (2)   (3)   (4)   (5)

3 First, listen to the following examples. Then, listen to the questions on the audio and answer them correctly. ▶ track **087**

(1)    (2)

(3)     (4)

 **Let's Study!**

Listen Listen and pay attention to the colored vowels of the following words. ▶track 088

(1) 야 구 ➡ ㅑ

(2) 요 가 ➡ ㅛ

(3) 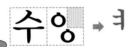 수 영 ➡ ㅕ

Learn The following four [y] vowels are formed by adding [y] before the basic vowels. Listen and repeat the audio. ▶track 089

(ㅑ) **[ya] as in yard**
Pronounce 'ㅑ' by pronouncing [y] and then immediately pronouncing 'ㅏ'.

(ㅕ) **[yeo] as in yawn**
Pronounce 'ㅕ' by pronouncing [y] and then immediately pronouncing 'ㅓ'. As with 'ㅓ', don't purse your lips. Don't pronounce it strongly.

(ㅛ) **[yo] as in yoga**
Pronounce 'ㅛ' by pronouncing [y] and then immediately pronouncing 'ㅗ'.

(ㅠ) **[yu] as in you**
Pronounce 'ㅠ' by pronouncing [y] and then immediately pronouncing 'ㅜ'.

---

[y] vowels

In Korean, the [y] vowels are pronounced the same as adding 'ㅣ' [y] before the basic vowels 'ㅏ, ㅓ, ㅗ, ㅜ'. Although the lips are shaped to pronounce [y], this sound is hardly pronounced. The pronunciation quickly changes to that of the basic vowels 'ㅏ, ㅓ, ㅗ, ㅜ'.

ㅣ + ㅏ = ㅑ
[y] [a] [ya]

Practice Listen and repeat the audio.

▶ track **090**

- With the mouth wide open

❶ With the [y] vowel

아 ➡ 야
[a]   [ya]

❷ With the [y] vowel

어 ➡ 여
[eo]   [yeo]

- With the lips pursed

❸ With the [y] vowel

오 ➡ 요
[o]   [yo]

❹ With the [y] vowel

우 ➡ 유
[u]   [yu]

✱ **Pronunciation Point**

1 It is difficult to differentiate between the pronunciations of the following. Look at the explanation and repeat the audio. ▶ track **091**

Ex.

요 여

Tip

Note the different shape of the mouth or lips.

요: Pronounce with the lips pursed.

여: Pronounce 'ㅛ' with the mouth open wide (but not as wide as when pronouncing 'ㅑ').

2 Listen and choose the correct answer. ▶ track **092**

(1) ⓐ 요리 ☐
    ⓑ 유리 ☐

(2) ⓐ 요기 ☐
    ⓑ 여기 ☐

(3) ⓐ 요가 ☐
    ⓑ 여가 ☐

(4) ⓐ 용 ☐
    ⓑ 영 ☐

Practice

1 When the consonant is written before the vowels 'ㅑ, ㅕ, ㅛ, ㅠ', the syllable is pronounced as follows. ▶track **093**

❶ With 'ㄴ' before 'ㅑ'

야 ➡ 냐
[ya]　　[nya]

❷ With 'ㅂ' before 'ㅕ'

여 ➡ 벼
[yeo]　　[byeo]

❸ With 'ㅁ' before 'ㅛ'

요 ➡ 묘
[yo]　　[myo]

❹ With 'ㄱ' before 'ㅠ'

유 ➡ 규
[yu]　　[gyu]

2 When 'ㅅ' comes before the vowels 'ㅑ, ㅕ, ㅛ, ㅠ', the pronunciation of 'ㅅ' changes from [s] to [sh]. ▶track **094**

❶ With 'ㅅ' before 'ㅑ'

사 ➡ 샤
[sa]　　[sha]

❷ With 'ㅅ' before 'ㅛ'

소 ➡ 쇼
[so]　　[sho]

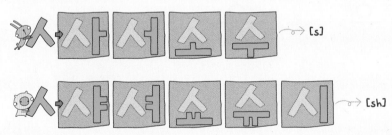

Tip 'ㅅ' is pronounced as [sh] when it is before the vowels 'ㅣ, ㅑ, ㅕ, ㅛ, ㅠ'.

Reading Activity!

1 Read the following. Listen and repeat the audio. ▶track 095

| (1) | 야 여
요 유 | (2) | 갸 겨
교 규 | (3) | 샤 셔
쇼 슈 | (4) | 약 역
욕 육 |

2 Listen and mark O if correct or X if incorrect. ▶track 096

(1) 양 ( )   (2) 병 ( )   (3) 교 ( )   (4) 류 ( )   (5) 형 ( )

3 Listen and choose the correct answer. ▶track 097

(1) ⓐ 약 ☐ ⓑ 역 ☐   (2) ⓐ 연기 ☐ ⓑ 용기 ☐

(3) ⓐ 별 ☐ ⓑ 벌 ☐   (4) ⓐ 귤 ☐ ⓑ 굴 ☐

(5) ⓐ 중요 ☐ ⓑ 조용 ☐   (6) ⓐ 요금 ☐ ⓑ 요즘 ☐

(7) ⓐ 목욕 ☐ ⓑ 모욕 ☐   (8) ⓐ 근면 ☐ ⓑ 금연 ☐

4 Listen and number the words in order. ▶track 098

무료	경기	공연
현금	서양	연구
학교	노력	기념

5 Listen and number the words in order. ▶track **099**

우유 ☐　　　중요 ☐　　　여자 ☐　　　수요일 ☐

씨유 ☐　　　씨름 ☐　　　양발 ☐　　　일요일 ☐

무역 ☐　　　안경 ☐　　　영어 ☐　　　주유소 ☐

6 Listen and choose the correct answer to complete the word. ▶track **100**

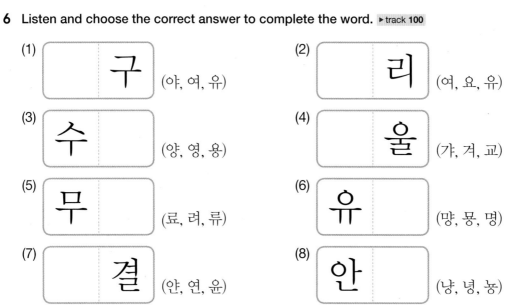

(1) ☐ 구　(야, 여, 유)

(2) ☐ 리　(여, 요, 유)

(3) 수 ☐　(양, 영, 용)

(4) ☐ 울　(갸, 겨, 교)

(5) 무 ☐　(료, 려, 류)

(6) 유 ☐　(먕, 뭉, 명)

(7) ☐ 결　(얀, 연, 윤)

(8) 안 ☐　(냥, 녕, 뇽)

7 Listen and match the picture with the word. ▶track **101**

(1) •　　　　　　　ⓐ 양복

(2) •　　　　　　　ⓑ 주유소

(3) •　　　　　　　ⓒ 수염

(4) •　　　　　　　ⓓ 저녁

★ Special Pronunciation Rule

Learn If 'ㅁ, ㄴ' is the initial sound of the syllable following the final consonants [ㅂ, ㄷ, ㄱ], then the pronunciation of the final consonants [ㅂ, ㄷ, ㄱ] change to [ㅁ, ㄴ, ㅇ], respectively. ▶track 102

(1) The pronunciation of the final consonant [ㅂ] changes to [ㅁ] when it is before the consonants 'ㅁ, ㄴ'.

Ex.

(2) The final consonants 'ㄷ, ㅅ, ㅈ' are pronounced as [ㄷ]. The pronunciation of the final consonant [ㄷ] changes to [ㄴ] when it is before the consonants 'ㅁ, ㄴ'.

Ex.

(3) The pronunciation of the final consonant [ㄱ] changes to [ㅇ] when it is before the consonants 'ㅁ, ㄴ'.

Ex.

Practice Listen and number the words in order. ▶track 103

Writing Activity!

The stroke order for writing vowels

▸ The stroke order is to write from top to bottom, and from left to right.

 A syllable with 'ㅁ, ㅂ' followed by the vowels 'ㅕ, ㅛ' can be difficult to read when the consonants and vowels are connected. These syllables can be easier to read if you first locate the vowel. Let's practice leaving a space between the consonants and vowels.

1 Listen and repeat the following syllables after the audio. Write them in the correct stroke order. ▸track **104**

(1)   (2)   (3)

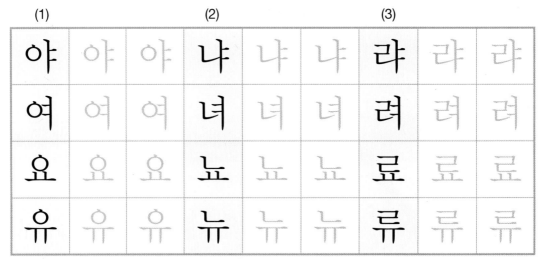

2 Listen and complete the word. ▸track **105**

(1)
(2)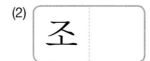
(3)

(4)
(5)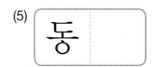
(6)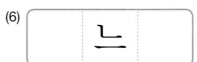

(7) 습
(8)
(9)

3 Listen and write the word. ►track 106

약

medicine

여자

woman

병

bottle

우유

milk

요리

cooking

영어

English

안경

glasses

유명

fame

1 Listen and fill in the words you hear. ▶ track **107**

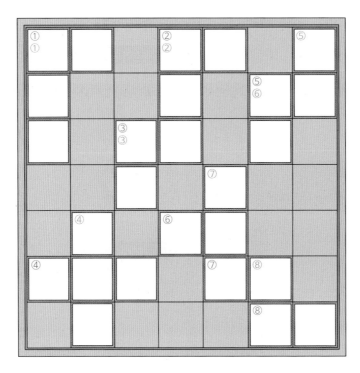

Across

① beard

② spare time

③ summer

④ Westerner

⑤ glasses

⑥ freedom

⑦ ownership

⑧ Myeongdong, a place of interest in downtown Seoul

Down

① a commission fee

② acne

③ woman

④ cat

⑤ night view

⑥ hello/bye

⑦ gas station

⑧ fame

2 Listen and complete the word. ▶track 108

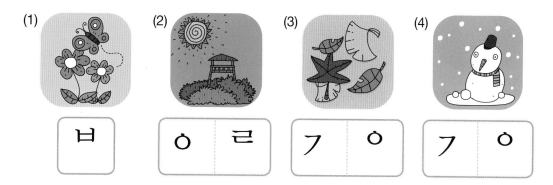

(1) ㅂ

(2) ㅇ ㄹ

(3) ㄱ ㅇ

(4) ㄱ ㅇ

3 Listen and choose the correct answer. ▶track 109

6

Two Basic Vowels ㅐ ㅔ
& Two [y] Vowels ㅒ ㅖ

Let's Warm Up!

1 Listen and repeat the following in order. ▶track **110**

2 Listen and write the letter you hear based on the pictures above. ▶track **111**

(1) (2) (3) (4) (5)

3 First, listen to the following examples. Then, listen to the questions on the audio and answer them correctly. ▶track **112**

(1)  (2)

(3)  (4)

Let's Study!

▶ track 113

Listen Listen and pay attention to the colored vowels of the following words.

(1)  새 우 ➡ ㅐ

(2)  조 개 ➡ ㅐ

(3)  게 ➡ ㅔ

(4)  계 란 ➡ ㅖ

Learn The following are two basic vowels and two [y] vowels. Listen and repeat the audio.

▶ track **114**

(ㅐ) **[ae] as in cat and pat**
Similar to the sound of [ae] in English. The mouth should be opened a bit wider than when pronouncing 'ㅔ'. Pronounce it strongly.

(ㅔ) **[e] as in end and pen**
Similar to the sound of [e] in English.

(ㅒ) **[yae] as in yak and yap**
Pronounce 'ㅒ' by starting with [y] and immediately pronouncing 'ㅐ'. Although the lips are shaped to pronounce [y], this sound is hardly pronounced. The pronunciation quickly changes to that of [ae].

(ㅖ) **[ye] as in yes and yet**
Pronounce 'ㅖ' by starting with [y] and immediately pronouncing 'ㅔ'. Although the lips are shaped to pronounce [y], this sound is hardly pronounced. The pronunciation quickly changes to that of [e].

Basic vowels 'ㅐ, ㅔ'

The vowel 'ㅐ' is formed by combining two basic vowels (ㅏ + ㅣ → ㅐ), while the vowel 'ㅔ' is formed by combining two basic vowels (ㅓ + ㅣ → ㅔ). The vowels 'ㅐ, ㅔ' are pronounced as the basic vowels [ae] and [e].

Pronunciation Tip Phonetically speaking, 'ㅐ, ㅔ' have different pronunciations, but they are pronounced almost the same.

Ex.  애 = 에
[ae]   [e]

Practice Listen and repeat the audio. 'ㅐ, ㅔ' are pronounced similarly. ▶track **115**

❶ With the [y] vowel in front of 'ㅐ'

 애 ➡ 애
[ae]   [yae]

❷ With the [y] vowel in front of 'ㅔ'

 에 ➡ 예
[e]   [ye]

✱ Pronunciation Point

'ㅐ, ㅔ' have similar pronunciations, but when used in words such as the following, they have completely different meanings. Therefore, you need to be careful with the spelling. The same applies for the vowels 'ㅒ, ㅖ'. ▶track **116**

❶ 개

dog

게

crab

❷  모래

sand

 모레

the day after tomorrow

1 Read the following. Listen and repeat the audio. ▶track 117

(1)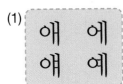

(2) 개 게
개 계

(3) 내 네
내 녜

(4) 래 레
래 례

2 Listen and mark O if correct or X if incorrect. ▶track 118

(1)
( )

(2) 배
( )

(3) 예
( )

(4) 셈
( )

(5)
( )

(6) 해
( )

(7) 계
( )

(8) 애
( )

3 Listen and choose the correct answer. ▶track 119

(1) ⓐ 아내 □ ⓑ 안내 □

(2) ⓐ 아래 □ ⓑ 안에 □

(3) ⓐ 어제 □ ⓑ 이제 □

(4) ⓐ 예순 □ ⓑ 예술 □

(5) ⓐ 재미 □ ⓑ 제비 □

(6) ⓐ 세계 □ ⓑ 시계 □

(7) ⓐ 여기 □ ⓑ 얘기 □

(8) ⓐ 계단 □ ⓑ 계산 □

4 Listen and number the words in order. ▶track **120**

내일 ☐　　숙제 ☐　　인생 ☐　　남동생 ☐

문제 ☐　　세상 ☐　　가게 ☐　　제주도 ☐

얘기 ☐　　계속 ☐　　예약 ☐　　냉장고 ☐

5 Listen and choose the correct answer to complete the word. ▶track **121**

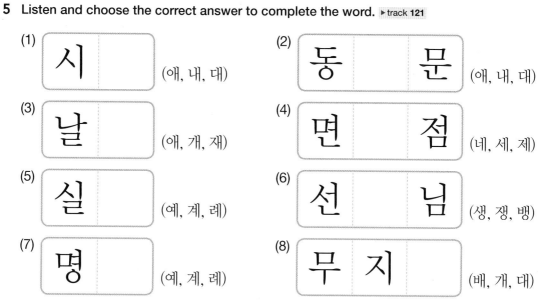

(1) 시 ☐　(애, 내, 대)

(2) 동 ☐ 문　(애, 내, 대)

(3) 날 ☐　(애, 개, 재)

(4) 면 ☐ 점　(네, 세, 제)

(5) 실 ☐　(예, 계, 례)

(6) 선 ☐ 님　(생, 쟁, 뱅)

(7) 명 ☐　(예, 계, 례)

(8) 무 지 ☐　(배, 개, 대)

6 Listen and match the picture with the word. ▶track **122**

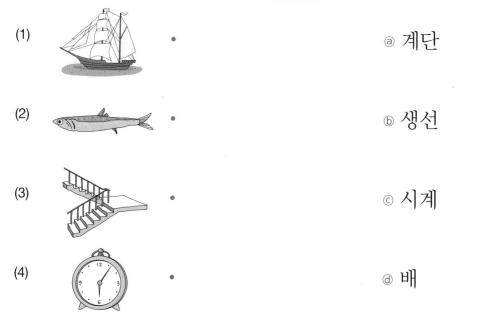

(1)　　　　•　　　•　ⓐ 계단

(2)　　　　•　　　•　ⓑ 생선

(3)　　　　•　　　•　ⓒ 시계

(4)　　　　•　　　•　ⓓ 배

7   Listen and number the words in order. ▶ track **123**

생일 　세계 　소개 　매일

기대 　재미 　경제 　오래

반대 　예상 　계절 　생각

★ **Special Pronunciation Rule**

Learn 'ㄴ' is pronounced as [ㄹ] when it comes before or after 'ㄹ'. ▶ track **124**

Ex. 신라 [실라]　　　　설날 [설랄]

Practice Listen and number the words in order. ▶ track **125**

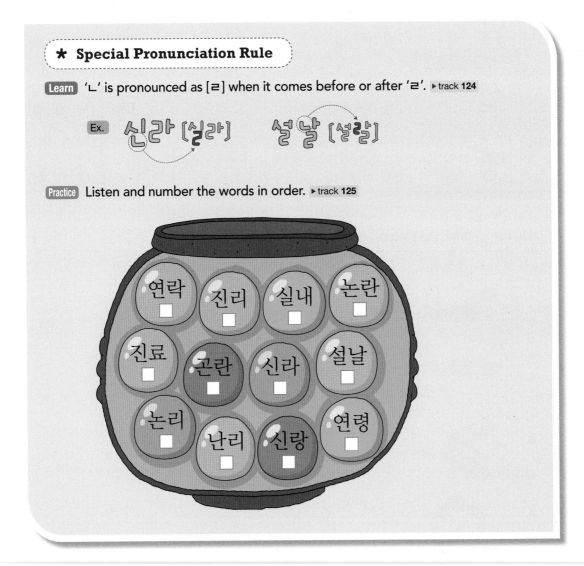

연락 　진리 　실내 　논란

진료 　곤란 　신라 　설날

논리 　난리 　신랑 　연령

The stroke order for writing vowels

▸ The stroke order is to write from top to bottom, and from left to right.

 Tip

The following syllables can be difficult to read when the consonants and vowels are connected. These syllables can be easier to read if you first locate the vowel. Let's practice leaving a space between the consonants and vowels.

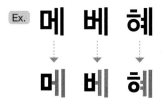

1 Listen and repeat the following syllables after the audio. Write them in the correct stroke order. ▸track **126**

(1)			(2)			(3)		
애	애	애	개	개	개	래	래	래
얘	얘	얘	걔	걔	걔	럐	럐	럐
에	에	에	게	게	게	레	레	레
예	예	예	계	계	계	례	례	례

2 Listen and write the word. ▶track 127

노래 _____ · song

맥주 _____ · beer

계단 _____ · stairs

베개 _____ · pillow

냄새 _____ · a smell

벌레 _____ · bug

비행기 _____ · airplane

냉장고 _____ · fridge

Quiz Yourself!

Listen and follow the path of the words you hear. Write the letter you arrive at. ▶track **128**

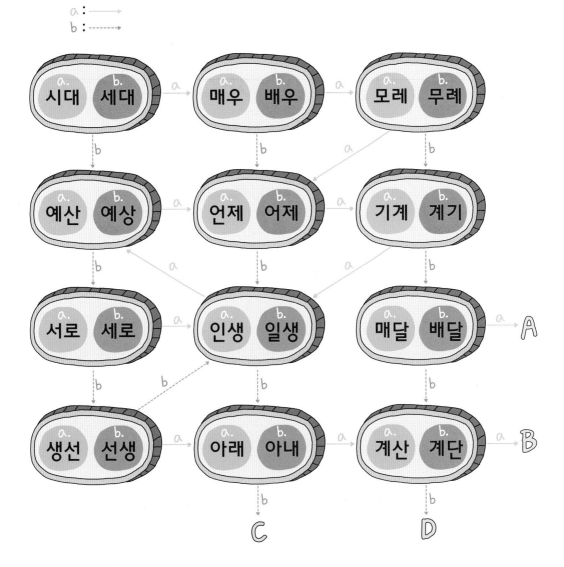

Final Answer: _____

Four Aspirated Consonants

ㅍ ㅌ ㅊ ㅋ

Let's Warm Up!

1 Listen and repeat the following in order. ▶ track **129**

ⓐ   ⓑ   ⓒ   ⓓ

ⓔ   ⓕ   ⓖ   ⓗ

2 Listen and write the letter you hear based on the pictures above. ▶ track **130**

(1)   (2)   (3)   (4)   (5)

3 First, listen to the following example. Then, practice how to order drinks. ▶ track **131**

Ex.
Please ...

(1) Please ...

(2) Please ...

(3) Please ...

Listen Listen and pay attention to the colored consonants of the following words.

▶ track **132**

(1)  ➡ ㅋ

(2) 커 ㅣ ➡ ㅍ

(3) 녹 ㅏ ➡ ㅊ

(4)  ㅣ ➡ ㅌ

Learn The following four consonants are all aspirated. You can feel a strong puff of air when they are pronounced.

ㅍ **[p] as in peace**
'ㅍ' is pronounced similar to [p] in English, that is, by releasing a puff of air when it is pronounced as the first sound of a syllable. In Korean, 'ㅍ' is pronounced more strongly than 'p' in English.

ㅌ **[t] as in teacher**
'ㅌ' is pronounced similar to [t] in English, that is, by releasing a puff of air when it is pronounced as the first sound of a syllable. In Korean, 'ㅌ' is pronounced more strongly than 't' in English.

ㅊ **[ch] as in chicken**
'ㅊ' is pronounced similar to [ch] in English when it is pronounced as the first sound of a syllable. In English, 'ch' is pronounced with the lips pursed whereas in Korean the lips take on the shape of the vowel that 'ㅊ' is written with. For example, if the vowel 'ㅏ' follows 'ㅊ', it is pronounced with the mouth wide open, but if the vowel 'ㅣ' follows 'ㅊ', it is pronounced with the lips stretched wide.

ㅋ **[k] as in kitchen**
'ㅋ' is pronounced similar to [k] in English, that is, by releasing a puff of air when it is pronounced as the first sound of a syllable. In Korean, 'ㅋ' is pronounced more strongly than 'k' in English.

Aspirated consonants are formed by adding strokes to the basic consonants

Aspirated consonants are formed by adding strokes to the basic consonants and are pronounced in the same tongue positions. Aspirated consonants 'ㅍ, ㅌ, ㅊ, ㅋ' are pronounced when 'ㅎ' is combined with the basic consonants 'ㅂ, ㄷ, ㅈ, ㄱ'.

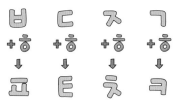

Practice Listen and repeat the basic and aspirated consonants. ▶ track 133

Basic	Aspirated

❶

바 [ba] ➡ 파 [pa]

❷

다 [da] ➡ 타 [ta]

❸

자 [ja] ➡ 차 [cha]

❹

가 [ga] ➡ 카 [ka]

Pronunciation Tip

Make sure you release a puff of air when you pronounce aspirated consonants!

The best way to practice pronouncing aspirated consonants is to hold a thin sheet of paper close to your lips so that you can "visually see" the puff of air. If you do this, you should see the paper move a lot when pronouncing the aspirated 파, but it will hardly move when pronouncing the basic 바.

★ Pronunciation Point

The following pairs of words differ by a single consonant. These words look similar, but you need to be careful of their different pronunciations and meanings. When aspirated consonants are pronounced, you can feel the air passage open wide as air is expelled more so than when basic consonants are pronounced. ▶ track **134**

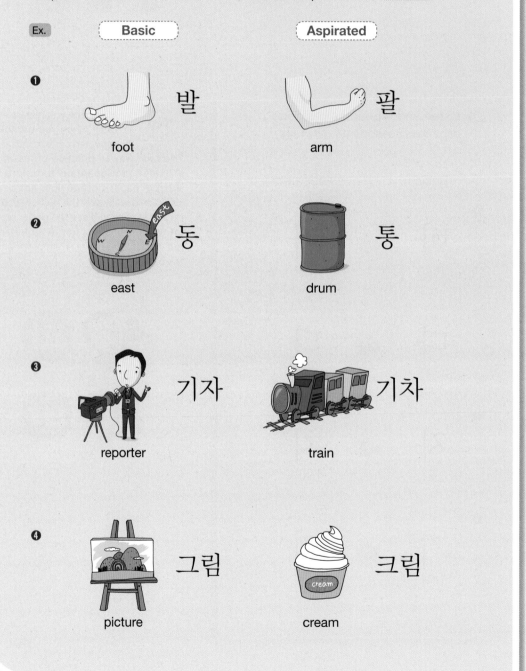

Ex.	**Basic**	**Aspirated**
❶	발 foot	팔 arm
❷	동 east	통 drum
❸	기자 reporter	기차 train
❹	그림 picture	크림 cream

 **Reading Activity!**

1 The following are basic consonants and aspirated consonants written side by side. Read the following. Listen and repeat the audio. ▶track **135**

(1)
바	파
버	퍼
보	포
부	푸
브	프
비	피

(2)
다	타
더	터
도	토
두	투
드	트
디	티

(3)
자	차
저	처
조	초
주	추
즈	츠
지	치

(4)
가	카
거	커
고	코
구	쿠
그	크
기	키

2 Listen and mark O if correct or X if incorrect. ▶track **136**

(1) 팔 ( ) 　(2) 턱 ( ) 　(3) 춤 ( ) 　(4) 콩 ( ) 　(5) 피 ( )

(6) 탕 ( ) 　(7) 키 ( ) 　(8) 틈 ( ) 　(9) 충 ( ) 　(10) 표 ( )

3 Listen and choose the correct answer. ▶track **137**

(1) ⓐ 보도 □　ⓑ 포도 □　　(2) ⓐ 자요 □　ⓑ 차요 □

(3) ⓐ 동기 □　ⓑ 통기 □　　(4) ⓐ 반사 □　ⓑ 판사 □

(5) ⓐ 다기 □　ⓑ 타기 □　　(6) ⓐ 저음 □　ⓑ 처음 □

(7) ⓐ 저리 □　ⓑ 처리 □　　(8) ⓐ 그림 □　ⓑ 크림 □

4 Listen and number the words in order. ▶ track **138**

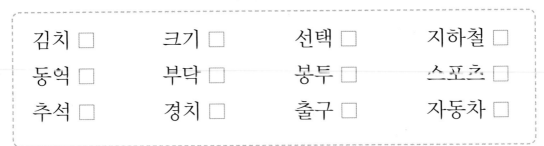

김치 ☐	크기 ☐	선택 ☐	지하철 ☐
동억 ☐	부닥 ☐	봉투 ☐	스포츠 ☐
추석 ☐	경치 ☐	출구 ☐	자동차 ☐

5 Listen and choose the correct answer to complete the word. ▶ track **139**

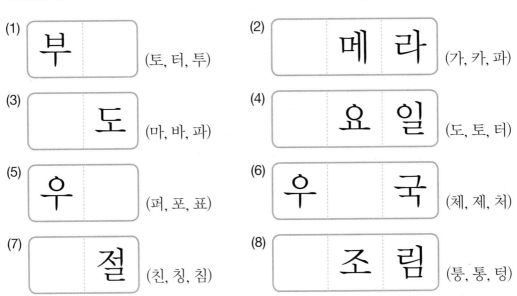

(1) 부 ☐☐ (토, 터, 투)

(2) 메 라 (가, 카, 파)

(3) ☐ 도 (마, 바, 파)

(4) 요 일 (도, 토, 터)

(5) 우 ☐ (퍼, 포, 표)

(6) 우 국 (체, 제, 처)

(7) ☐ 절 (친, 칭, 침)

(8) 조 림 (퉁, 통, 텅)

6 Listen and match the picture with the word. ▶ track **140**

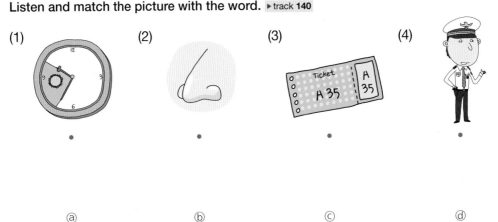

(1)　　　　(2)　　　　(3)　　　　(4)

　·　　　　·　　　　·　　　　·

ⓐ 표　　　ⓑ 아침　　　ⓒ 코　　　ⓓ 경찰

★ Special Pronunciation Rule

Learn 'ㅎ' makes aspirated consonants when combined with the following consonants. ▶track 141

(1) If 'ㅎ' is the initial sound of the syllable following the final consonants 'ㅂ, ㄷ, ㅈ, ㄱ', then the sounds of 'ㅎ' and the final consonant combine. The sound of the final consonants 'ㅂ, ㄷ, ㅈ, ㄱ' changes to [ㅍ, ㅌ, ㅊ, ㅋ], respectively.

Ex.

(2) If the final consonant 'ㅎ' is followed by 'ㅂ, ㄷ, ㅈ, ㄱ', 'ㅎ' combines with these consonants to make their respective aspirated consonants [ㅍ, ㅌ, ㅊ, ㅋ].

Ex.

Practice

1 Listen and number the words in order. ▶track 142

입학 ☐　　　놓다 ☐　　　육 호선 ☐　　　이렇게 ☐

맏형 ☐　　　좋고 ☐　　　못해요 ☐　　　그렇지 ☐

2 Listen and choose the correct answer to complete the word. ▶track 143

(1) 연 ☐ 해 요 (슥, 슴, 습)

(2) 생 ☐ 해 요 (각, 갑, 갓)

(3) 행 ☐ 해 요 (복, 봄, 봅)

(4) 비 ☐ 해 요 (슴, 습, 슷)

Writing Activity!

The stroke order for writing consonants

▸ The stroke order is to write from top to bottom, and from left to right.

 There may be times when it is difficult to read 표 or 터 because there is no space between the consonant and vowel in the written form. These syllables can be easily read if you first locate the vowel. Let's practice leaving a space between the consonants and vowels.

Ex. **표 터**

 When the consonant '**ㅋ**' is followed by a vertical vowel (ㅏ, ㅓ, ㅣ, etc.), it is written as '**ㅋ**' the same way as '**ㄱ**'.

Ex. (straight) 코 쿠 크
(curving) 카 커 키

1 Listen and repeat the following syllables after the audio. Write them in the correct stroke order. ▸track **144**

(3)   (4)

2 Listen and complete the word. ▶track 145

(1)  도

(2) 보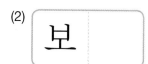

(3) 김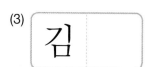

(4) 남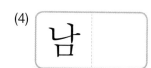

(5)  발

(6) 도

(7) 연

(8) 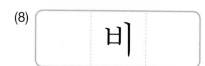 비

(9) 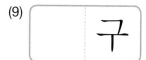 구

(10) 퓨

3 Listen and write the word. ▶track 146

자동차

car

주차장

parking lot

지하철

subway

택시

taxi

기차

train

선풍기

electric fan

자판기

vending machine

세탁기

washer

코
nose

표
ticket

책
book

친구
friend

아침
morning

핸드폰
mobile phone

침대
bed

단추
button

Quiz Yourself!

1 Listen and choose the correct answer. ▶track **147**

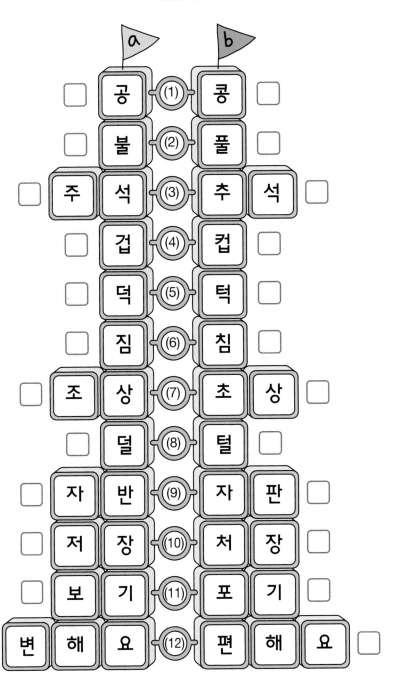

a		b
공	(1)	콩
불	(2)	풀
주 석	(3)	추 석
겁	(4)	컵
덕	(5)	턱
짐	(6)	침
조 상	(7)	초 상
덜	(8)	털
자 반	(9)	자 판
저 장	(10)	처 장
보 기	(11)	포 기
변 해 요	(12)	편 해 요

2 Listen and complete the word. ▶track **148**

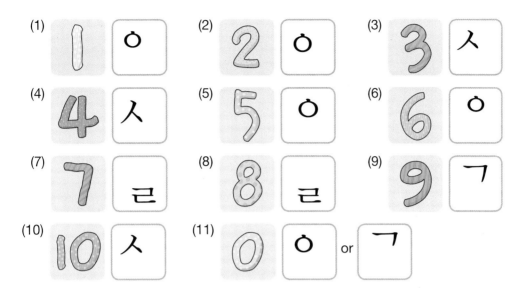

(1) 1 ㅇ   (2) 2 ㅇ   (3) 3 ㅅ

(4) 4 ㅅ   (5) 5 ㅇ   (6) 6 ㅇ

(7) 7 ㄹ   (8) 8 ㄹ   (9) 9 ㄱ

(10) 10 ㅅ   (11) 0 ㅇ or ㄱ

3 Listen and number the words in order. ▶track **149**

삼촌　칭찬　만큼　배추　에어컨　스키
경찰　교통　피부　핸드폰　택시　커피　책
녹차　처음　표　사촌　통역　평일
카메라　추억　청소　풀　칠판

4 Listen and complete the names of the countries you hear. Check them with the numbers on the map. ▶track **150**

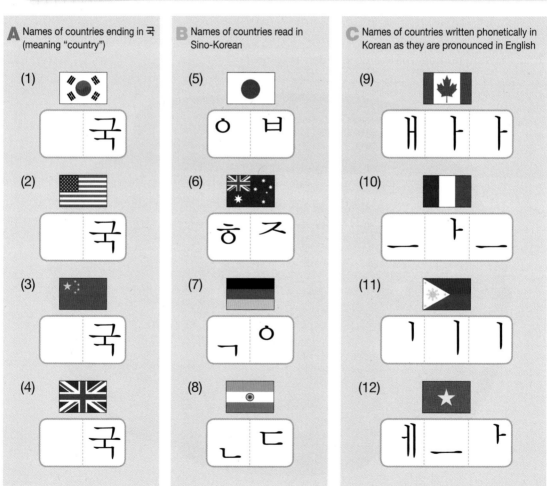

5 Listen and complete Seoul's hot spots based on the subway line map. ▶track 151

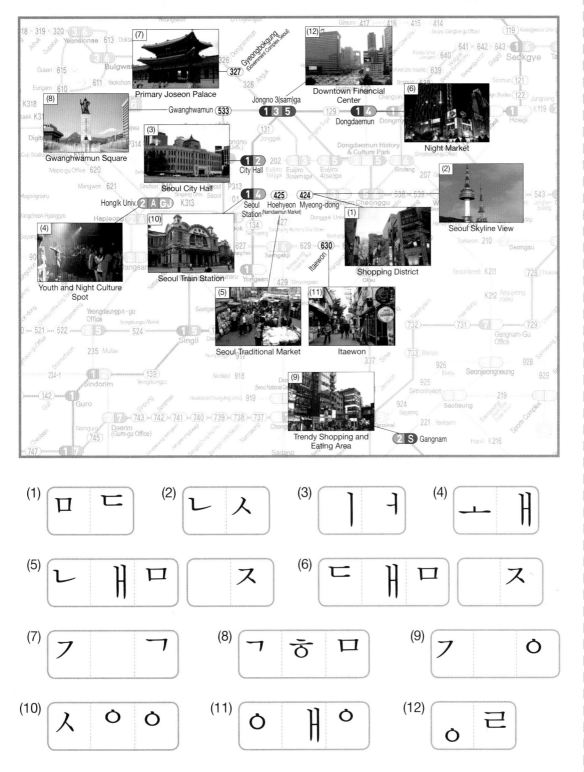

(1)
ㅁ	ㄷ

(2)
ㄴ	ㅅ

(3)
ㅣ	ㅓ

(4)
ㅗ	ㅐ

(5)
ㄴ	ㅐ	ㅁ	ㅈ

(6)
ㄷ	ㅐ	ㅁ	ㅈ

(7)
ㄱ	ㄱ

(8)
ㄱ	ㅎ	ㅁ

(9)
ㄱ	ㅇ

(10)
ㅅ	ㅇ	ㅇ

(11)
ㅇ	ㅐ	ㅇ

(12)
ㅇ	ㄹ

Seven Compound Vowels

과 궈 괘 궤 괴 귀 긔

 Let's Warm Up!

1 Listen and repeat the following in order. ▶ track **152**

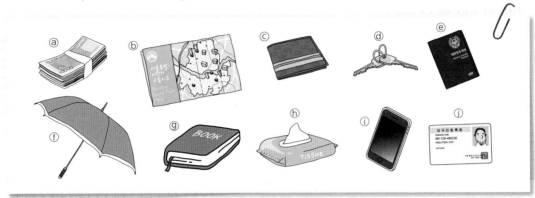

2 Listen and write the letter you hear based on the pictures above. ▶ track **153**

(1) (2) (3) (4) (5) (6)

3 First, listen to the following examples. Then, listen to the questions on the audio and answer them correctly. ▶ track **154**

(1)
(2)

(3)
(4)

Let's Study!

Listen Listen and pay attention to the colored vowels of the following words. ▶track 155

(1)  외 국 인 등 록 증 → ㅚ

(2) 열 쇠 → ㅚ (3) 여권 → ㅝ

Learn The following are seven compound vowels. ▶track 156

There are six [w] compound vowels 'ㅘ, ㅝ, ㅙ, ㅞ, ㅚ, ㅟ' and the compound vowel 'ㅢ'. Aside from 'ㅢ', the sound of [w] is added before the other six compound vowels. As in pronouncing 'ㅗ, ㅜ', these vowels are pronounced with the lips initially pursed.

ㅘ [wa] **as in wine**
'ㅘ' is pronounced by adding the sound of [w] before the vowel 'ㅏ'. Start with the lips shaped to pronounce 'ㅗ' and very quickly change to 'ㅏ'.

ㅝ [weo] **as in walk**
'ㅝ' is pronounced by adding the sound of [w] before the vowel 'ㅓ'. Start with the lips shaped to pronounce 'ㅜ' and very quickly change to 'ㅓ'.

ㅙ [wae] **as in wag** (American)
'ㅙ' is pronounced by adding the sound of [w] before the vowel 'ㅐ'. Start with the lips shaped to pronounce 'ㅗ' and very quickly change to 'ㅐ'.

ㅞ [we] **as in wedding**
'ㅞ' is pronounced by adding the sound of [w] before the vowel 'ㅔ'. Start with the lips shaped to pronounce 'ㅜ' and very quickly change to 'ㅔ'.

ㅚ [oe] **as in weight**
'ㅚ' is actually pronounced similar to 'ㅞ' [we].

ㅟ [wi] **as in we**
'ㅟ' is pronounced by adding the sound of [w] before the vowel 'ㅣ'. Start with the lips shaped to pronounce 'ㅜ' and very quickly change to 'ㅣ'.

ㅢ [ui] **as in gooey**
Start with the lips shaped to pronounce 'ㅡ' and very quickly change to 'ㅣ'.

As illustrated below, compound vowels are the vowel sounds that result from quickly pronouncing two vowels combined together. Listen and repeat the audio. ▸track **157**

❶

오 ✚ 아 ➡ 와
[o]　　[a]　　[wa]

❷

우 ✚ 어 ➡ 워
[u]　　[eo]　　[weo]

❸

오 ✚ 애 ➡ 왜
[o]　　[ae]　　[wae]

❹

우 ✚ 에 ➡ 웨
[u]　　[e]　　[we]

❺

오 ✚ 이 ➡ 외
[o]　　[y]　　[oe]

❻

우 ✚ 이 ➡ 위
[u]　　[y]　　[wi]

❼

으 ✚ 이 ➡ 의
[eu]　　[y]　　[eui]

Pronunciation **Tip**

These [w] compound vowels are pronounced by starting with the lips pursed.

✱ Pronunciation Point

1 The vowels '왜, 웨, 외' are spelled differently, but they actually have similar pronunciations. ▸track **158**

Ex.

2 Choose the underlined vowel that has a completely different pronunciation from the other two. Check the answer by listening to the audio. ▸track **159**

(1) ⓐ 왜 ☐
　　ⓑ 위기 ☐
　　ⓒ 외국 ☐

(2) ⓐ 열쇠 ☐
　　ⓑ 인쇄 ☐
　　ⓒ 부숴요 ☐

(3) ⓐ 전화 ☐
　　ⓑ 사회 ☐
　　ⓒ 훼손 ☐

(4) ⓐ 괴물 ☐
　　ⓑ 일궈요 ☐
　　ⓒ 궤도 ☐

★ Pronunciation Point

1 Six [w] compound vowels

The six [w] compound vowels are pronounced by starting with the lips pursed and pronouncing 'ㅗ' or 'ㅜ' and then adding a basic vowel sound.

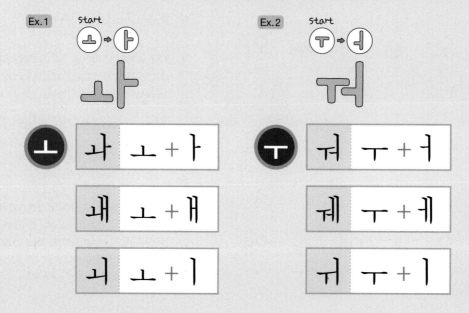

Ex. 1

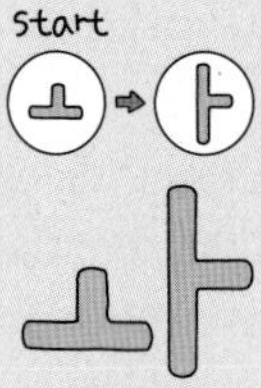

Ex. 2

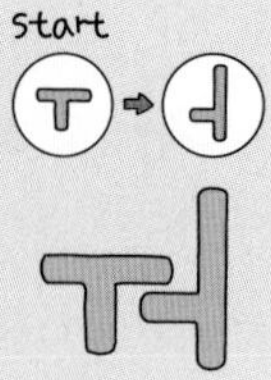

ㅗ

놔	ㅗ + ㅏ
놰	ㅗ + ㅐ
뇌	ㅗ + ㅣ

ㅜ

눠	ㅜ + ㅓ
눼	ㅜ + ㅔ
뉘	ㅜ + ㅣ

2 The vowel 'ㅢ'

The vowel 'ㅢ' is pronounced by pronouncing 'ㅡ' and 'ㅣ' as quickly as possible and as a single syllable.

Ex. 3

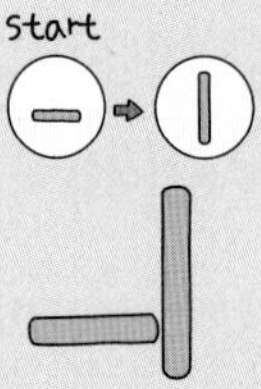

 **Reading Activity!**

1 Read the following. Listen and repeat the audio. ▶track **160**

(1)
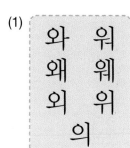

와	워
왜	웨
외	위
의	

(2)

과	귀
괘	궤
괴	귀
긔	

(3)

화	훠
홰	훼
회	휘
희	

2 Listen and mark O if correct or X if incorrect. ▶track **161**

(1) 　왜
( )

(2) 　위
( )

(3) 　과
( )

(4) 　회
( )

(5) 　뒤
( )

(6) 　귀
( )

(7) 　뇌
( )

(8) 　의
( )

(9) 　죄
( )

(10) 원
( )

3 Listen and choose the correct answer. ▶track **162**

(1) ⓐ 쇠 ☐　ⓑ 세 ☐

(2) ⓐ 사위 ☐　ⓑ 사회 ☐

(3) ⓐ 회 ☐　ⓑ 해 ☐

(4) ⓐ 이사 ☐　ⓑ 의사 ☐

(5) ⓐ 귀 ☐　ⓑ 뒤 ☐

(6) ⓐ 주위 ☐　ⓑ 주의 ☐

(7) ⓐ 뭐 ☐　ⓑ 뫼 ☐

(8) ⓐ 인세 ☐　ⓑ 인쇄 ☐

(9) ⓐ 죄 ☐　ⓑ 쥐 ☐

(10) ⓐ 외국 ☐　ⓑ 애국 ☐

4 Listen and number the words in order. ▶ track **163**

위험 ☐　　　취소 ☐　　　교회 ☐　　　추워요 ☐

병원 ☐　　　의견 ☐　　　영화 ☐　　　대사관 ☐

희망 ☐　　　최고 ☐　　　과일 ☐　　　매워요 ☐

5 Listen and choose the correct answer to complete the word. ▶ track **164**

(1) 사 ☐ (가, 과, 귀)

(2) 장 실 (하, 화, 회)

(3) 사 (회, 휘, 화)

(4) 더 요 (와, 위, 워)

(5) 사 (이, 으, 의)

(6) 회 전 (자, 좌, 줘)

(7) 지 (대, 돼, 뒤)

(8) 국 인 (에, 외, 의)

(9) 손 (화, 훼, 휘)

(10) 파 람 (회, 훼, 휘)

6 Listen and match the picture with the word. ▶ track **165**

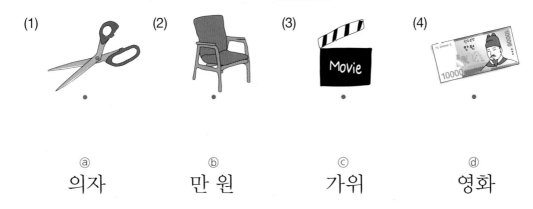

(1)　　　　　(2)　　　　　(3)　　　　　(4)

ⓐ 의자　　　ⓑ 만 원　　　ⓒ 가위　　　ⓓ 영화

★ Special Pronunciation Rule

Learn The vowel 'ㅢ' can be pronounced differently. ▶ track 166

(1) The vowel 'ㅢ' is always pronounced as 'ㅢ' when it is the first syllable of a word, but when written as the second syllable, it is pronounced as 'ㅢ' or 'ㅣ'. Let's practice the easier pronunciation of 'ㅣ'.

Ex.

의자 주의

(2) When a consonant is written in front of the vowel 'ㅢ', the pronunciation of 'ㅢ' becomes 'ㅣ'.

Ex.

희망 무늬

Practice Listen and number the words in order. ▶ track 167

Writing Activity!

The stroke order for writing vowels

▸ The stroke order is to write from top to bottom, and from left to right.

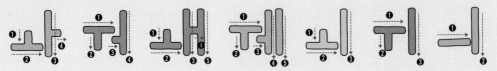

 The following is an example of vowels that have been written incorrectly. When writing
와, the horizontal stroke of '바' must be written higher than the vowel 'ㅗ'. When writing
the vowel 워, the horizontal stroke of '바' must be written lower than the vowel 'ㅜ'.

Ex.

1 Listen and repeat the following syllables after the audio. Write them in the correct stroke
order. ▸ track **168**

(1)			(2)			(3)		
와	와	와	과	과	과	화	화	화
워	워	워	궈	궈	궈	훠	훠	훠
왜	왜	왜	괘	괘	괘	홰	홰	홰
웨	웨	웨	궤	궤	궤	훼	훼	훼
외	외	외	괴	괴	괴	회	회	회
위	위	위	귀	귀	귀	휘	휘	휘
의	의	의	긔	긔	긔	희	희	희

2 Listen and complete the word. ▶ track **169**

(1) 영 ☐

(2) ☐ 자

(3) 외 ☐

(4) 주 ☐

(5) 돼 ☐

(6) 죄 ☐

(7) 희 ☐

(8) 외 ☐

(9) ☐ 심

(10) 영 ☐

(11) 분 ☐ 기

(12) ☐ 워 요

3 Listen and fill in the blank. ▶ track **170**

(1)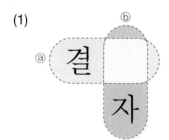

(2)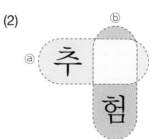

(3)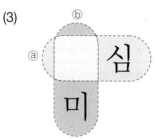

(4)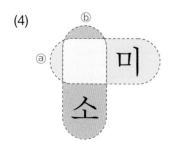

(5)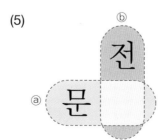

(6)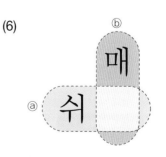

4 Listen and write the word. ▶ track 171

과일	전화
fruit	call
쥐	돼지
rat	pig
바위	바퀴
rock	wheel
영화	주의
movie	caution

Quiz Yourself!

1 Listen and complete the word. ▸track **172**

(1) Monday

| ㄹ | 요 | 일 |

(2) Tuesday

| ㅎ | 요 | 일 |

(3) Wednesday

| ㅅ | 요 | 일 |

(4) Thursday

| ㄱ | 요 | 일 |

(5) Friday

| ㅁ | 요 | 일 |

(6) Saturday

| ㅌ | 요 | 일 |

(7) Sunday

| ㄹ | 요 | 일 |

2 Look at the picture. Listen and write the word. ▸track **173**

(1)

(2)

(3)

(4)

(5)

(6)

(7)

(8)

(9)

3 Listen and follow the path of the words you hear. ▶ track 174

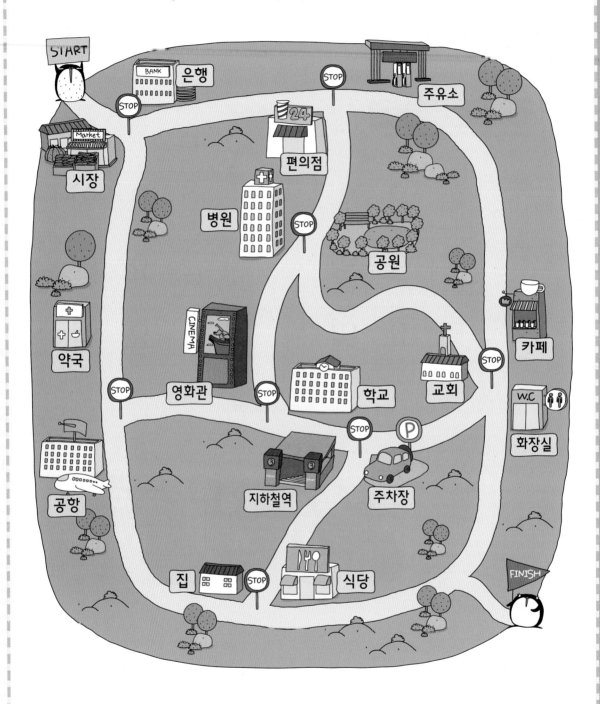

4 Listen and write the letter that matches the picture. ▶track **175**

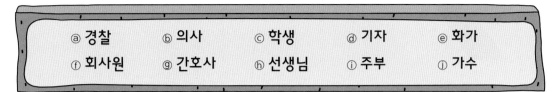

ⓐ 경찰　　ⓑ 의사　　ⓒ 학생　　ⓓ 기자　　ⓔ 화가
ⓕ 회사원　　ⓖ 간호사　　ⓗ 선생님　　ⓘ 주부　　ⓙ 가수

직업 (jobs)

(1)　(2)　(3)　(4)　(5)　(6)　(7)　(8)　(9)　(10)

Chapter

9

Five Tensed Consonants

ㅃ ㄸ ㅆ ㅉ ㄲ

Let's Warm Up!

1 Listen and repeat the following in order. ▶track 176

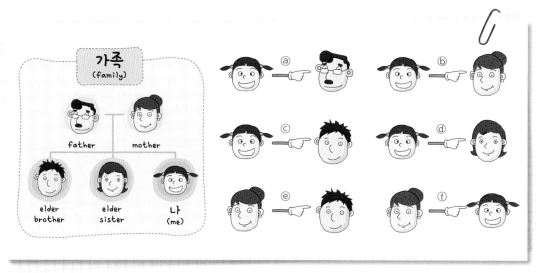

2 Listen and write the letter you hear based on the pictures above. ▶track 177

(1) ☐ (2) ☐ (3) ☐ (4) ☐ (5) ☐

3 First, listen to the following example. Then, listen to the questions on the audio and answer them correctly. ▶track 178

(1)

(2)

(3)

Let's Study!

▶ track 179

Listen Listen and pay attention to the colored consonants of the following words.

(1)

(2)

(3)

Learn The following five consonants are tensed sounds. These sounds are pronounced with the vocal cords closed and the air in the lungs compressed. After a little air is released, the vocal cords are quickly closed again.

ㅃ
[pp] as in "bad!"
The pronunciation of the Korean 'ㅃ' is similar to the sound of the stressed 'p' with more tension in the vocal cords.

ㄸ
[tt] as in "duh!"
The pronunciation of the Korean 'ㄸ' is similar to the sound of the stressed 't' with more tension in the vocal cords.

ㅆ
[ss] as in sang (with a strong pronunciation)
The pronunciation of the Korean 'ㅆ' is similar to the sound of the stressed 's' with more tension in the vocal cords.

ㅉ
[jj] as in "gotcha!"
The pronunciation of the Korean 'ㅉ' is similar to the sound of the stressed 'ch' in gotcha when it is pronounced strongly.

ㄲ
[kk] as in "gotcha!"
The pronunciation of the Korean 'ㄲ' is similar to the sound of the stressed 'g' in gotcha when it is pronounced strongly.

The formation of tensed consonants

Tensed consonants are formed by writing two basic consonants (that are pronounced in the same position) side by side.

Listen and repeat the basic consonants
and tensed consonants. ▶ track **180**

Basic	Tensed
❶ 바 ➡ 빠	
[ba]	[ppa]
❷ 다 ➡ 따	
[da]	[tta]
❸ 사 ➡ 싸	
[sa]	[ssa]
❹ 자 ➡ 짜	
[ja]	[jja]
❺ 가 ➡ 까	
[ga]	[kka]

Pronunciation
Tip

To pronounce tensed consonants, you
should stop the flow of breath after
releasing a very slight amount of air.
Don't release air from your mouth when
pronouncing tensed consonants. You
should be able to observe the following
when you hold a thin sheet of paper
in front of your mouth and practice
pronunciation.

Basic consonants
– The paper should move slightly.

Aspirated consonants
– The paper should move a lot.

Tensed consonants
– The paper shouldn't move at all.

✱ Pronunciation Point

The following words differ by a single consonant. These words look similar, but you need to be careful of their different pronunciations and meanings. ▶ track **181**

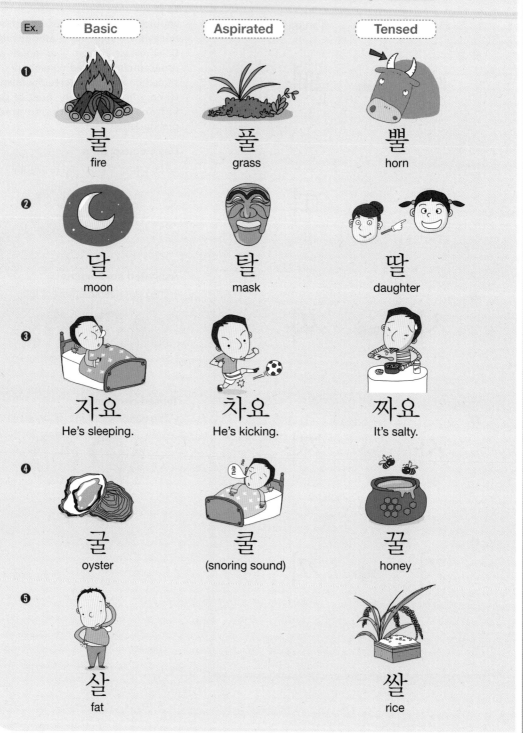

Ex.	Basic	Aspirated	Tensed
❶	불 fire	풀 grass	뿔 horn
❷	달 moon	탈 mask	딸 daughter
❸	자요 He's sleeping.	차요 He's kicking.	짜요 It's salty.
❹	굴 oyster	쿨 (snoring sound)	꿀 honey
❺	살 fat		쌀 rice

130 · Korean made easy · Starter (2nd edition)

Reading Activity!

1 Read the following. Listen and repeat the audio. ▶ track **182**

(1)
바	빠
버	뻐
보	뽀
부	뿌
브	쁘
비	삐

(2)
다	따
더	떠
도	또
두	뚜
드	뜨
디	띠

(3)
사	싸
서	써
소	쏘
수	쑤
스	쓰
시	씨

(4)
자	짜
저	쩌
조	쪼
주	쭈
즈	쯔
지	찌

(5)
가	까
거	꺼
고	꼬
구	꾸
그	끄
기	끼

2 Listen and mark O if correct or X if incorrect. ▶ track **183**

(1) 딸 ( )　(2) 찜 ( )　(3) 꼭 ( )　(4) 뿐 ( )　(5) 씨 ( )

(6) 뜻 ( )　(7) 꿈 ( )　(8) 쭉 ( )　(9) 쌀 ( )　(10) 빰 ( )

3 Listen and choose the correct answer. ▶ track **184**

(1) ⓐ 방 ☐　ⓑ 빵 ☐　　　　(2) ⓐ 대문 ☐　ⓑ 때문 ☐

(3) ⓐ 삼 ☐　ⓑ 쌈 ☐　　　　(4) ⓐ 가지 ☐　ⓑ 까지 ☐

(5) ⓐ 곡 ☐　ⓑ 꼭 ☐　　　　(6) ⓐ 사요 ☐　ⓑ 싸요 ☐

(7) ⓐ 벼 ☐　ⓑ 뼈 ☐　　　　(8) ⓐ 자리 ☐　ⓑ 짜리 ☐

4 Listen and number the words in order. ▶ track **185**

떡 ☐	뿌리 ☐	씨름 ☐	아저씨 ☐
짝 ☐	가끔 ☐	토끼 ☐	깨끗이 ☐
빵 ☐	눈썹 ☐	뚜껑 ☐	어쩐지 ☐

5 Listen and choose the correct answer to complete the word. ▶ track **186**

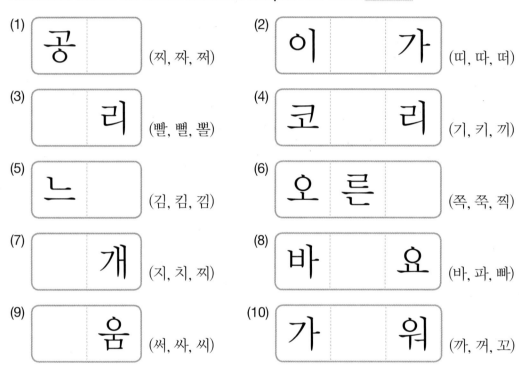

(1) 공 ☐ (찌, 짜, 쩌)

(2) 이 ☐ 가 (띠, 따, 떠)

(3) ☐ 리 (빨, 뻘, 뿔)

(4) 코 ☐ 리 (기, 키, 끼)

(5) ☐ 느 (김, 킴, 낌)

(6) 오 른 ☐ (쪽, 쭉, 찍)

(7) ☐ 개 (지, 치, 찌)

(8) 바 ☐ 요 (바, 파, 빠)

(9) ☐ 움 (써, 싸, 씨)

(10) 가 ☐ 워 (까, 꺼, 꼬)

6 Listen and match the picture with the word. ▶ track **187**

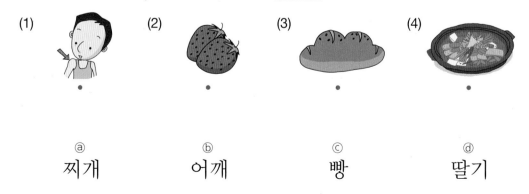

(1) ●   (2) ●   (3) ●   (4) ●

ⓐ 찌개   ⓑ 어깨   ⓒ 빵   ⓓ 딸기

★ Special Pronunciation Rule

Learn The pronunciations of the consonants 'ㅂ, ㄷ, ㅅ, ㅈ, ㄱ' change to [ㅃ, ㄸ, ㅆ, ㅉ, ㄲ], respectively, when they follow the pronunciations of [ㅂ, ㄷ, ㄱ] in the final consonant. ▶track 188

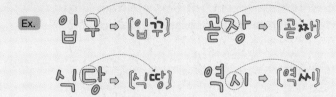

Ex. 입구 ➡ [입꾸]   곧장 ➡ [곧짱]

식당 ➡ [식땅]   역시 ➡ [역씨]

Practice

1 Listen and number the words in order. ▶track 189

목적 ☐	늦게 ☐	혹시 ☐	숟가락 ☐
역시 ☐	습관 ☐	집중 ☐	갑자기 ☐
옷장 ☐	덕분 ☐	각각 ☐	목소리 ☐

2 Listen and complete the word. ▶track 190

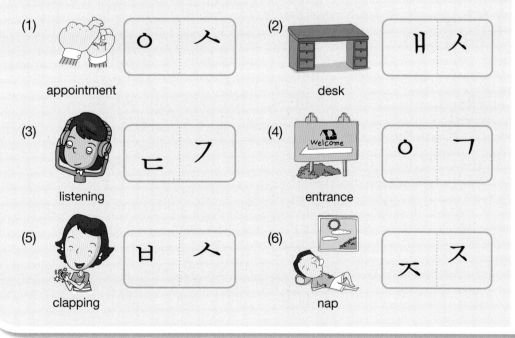

(1) ㅇ ㅅ
appointment

(2) ㅐ ㅅ
desk

(3) ㄷ ㄱ
listening

(4) ㅇ ㄱ
entrance

(5) ㅂ ㅅ
clapping

(6) ㅈ ㅈ
nap

Writing Activity!

The stroke order for writing consonants

▸ The stroke order is to write from top to bottom, and from left to right. Tensed consonants are formed by writing two basic consonants in a row from left to right.

Tip

In the case of the tensed consonant 'ㅃ', the two 'ㅂ' consonants may appear with or without a space between them depending on the font. They may look different, but they are the same. You should practice writing this tensed consonant with a space between the two 'ㅂ' consonants.

Ex.

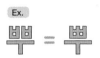

1 Listen and repeat the following syllables after the audio. Write them in the correct stroke order. ▸ track **191**

(1)			(2)			(3)		
빠	빠	빠	따	따	따	싸	싸	싸
뻐	뻐	뻐	떠	떠	떠	써	써	써
뽀	뽀	뽀	또	또	또	쏘	쏘	쏘
뿌	뿌	뿌	뚜	뚜	뚜	쑤	쑤	쑤
쁘	쁘	쁘	뜨	뜨	뜨	쓰	쓰	쓰
삐	삐	삐	띠	띠	띠	씨	씨	씨

(4) | | | (5) | |
---|---|---|---|---|---
짜 | 짜 | 짜 | 까 | 까 | 까
쩌 | 쩌 | 쩌 | 꺼 | 꺼 | 꺼
쪼 | 쪼 | 쪼 | 꼬 | 꼬 | 꼬
쭈 | 쭈 | 쭈 | 꾸 | 꾸 | 꾸
쯔 | 쯔 | 쯔 | 끄 | 끄 | 끄
찌 | 찌 | 찌 | 끼 | 끼 | 끼

2 Listen and complete the word. ▶track 192

(1) 자

(2) 솜

(3) 래

(4) 가

(5) 잠

(6) 비 요

(7) 깜

(8) 아 저

(9) 말

(10) 기 요

3 Listen and write the word. ▶ track **193**

꿈

dream

꼬리

tail

땀

sweat

뚜껑

cover

쓰레기통

garbage can

짜요

It's salty.

찜질방

sauna

오빠

(female's)
elder brother

쌍둥이 — **twins**	오른쪽 — **right**
빵 — **bread**	어깨 — **shoulder**
토끼 — **rabbit**	비싸요 — **It's expensive.**
떡 — **(Korean) rice cake**	공짜 — **free**

1 Listen and choose the correct answer. ▶ track **194**

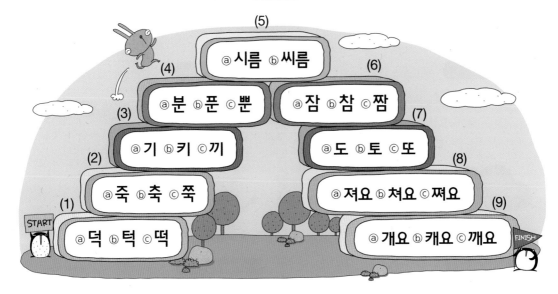

(5) ⓐ 시름 ⓑ 씨름

(4) ⓐ 분 ⓑ 푼 ⓒ 뿐

(6) ⓐ 잠 ⓑ 참 ⓒ 짬

(3) ⓐ 기 ⓑ 키 ⓒ 끼

(7) ⓐ 도 ⓑ 토 ⓒ 또

(2) ⓐ 죽 ⓑ 축 ⓒ 쭉

(8) ⓐ 져요 ⓑ 쳐요 ⓒ 쪄요

(1) ⓐ 덕 ⓑ 턱 ⓒ 떡

(9) ⓐ 개요 ⓑ 캐요 ⓒ 깨요

2 Listen and number the words in order. ▶ track **195**

빵집	글쎄	똑바로	쯤	일찍
벌써	짜증	쑥	따로	꼭지
싸움	나빠요	함께	손뼉	예뻐요
팔꿈치	뿌리	쓰기	꾸중	그때
진짜	깜짝	짜리	살짝	또

3 Look at the picture. Listen and complete the word. ▶track **196**

(1)

ㅏ	ㅘ

(2)

ㅐ

(3)

ㅏ	ㅣ

(4)

ㅗ	ㅗ

(5)

ㅜ	ㅏ

(6)

ㅏ	ㅏ	ㅏ

(7)

ㅏ

(8)

ㅠ

Final Consonants
ㅍ ㅌ ㅊ ㅋ ㅆ ㄲ
& Double Final Consonants

Let's Warm Up!

1 Listen and write the letter that matches the picture. ▶track **197**

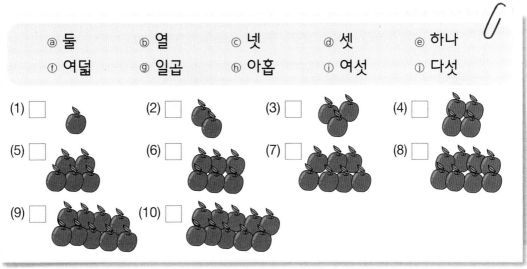

ⓐ 둘　　ⓑ 열　　ⓒ 넷　　ⓓ 셋　　ⓔ 하나
ⓕ 여덟　　ⓖ 일곱　　ⓗ 아홉　　ⓘ 여섯　　ⓙ 다섯

(1) ☐　　(2) ☐　　(3) ☐　　(4) ☐

(5) ☐　　(6) ☐　　(7) ☐　　(8) ☐

(9) ☐　　(10) ☐

2 Listen and match the picture with the word. ▶track **198**

(1) 　　•　　ⓐ 두 개

(2) 　　•　　ⓑ 세 개

(3) 　　•　　ⓒ 아홉 개

(4) 　　•　　ⓓ 여섯 개

Tip

개 is used as a counting unit for items. When counting, the numbers are used as follows. The numbers 1 to 4 change their forms before 개.

Ex.

하나 [hana]	⇨	한 개 [han gae]
둘 [dul]	⇨	두 개 [du gae]
셋 [set]	⇨	세 개 [se gae]
넷 [net]	⇨	네 개 [ne gae]
다섯	⇨	다섯 개
여섯	⇨	여섯 개
일곱	⇨	일곱 개
여덟	⇨	여덟 개
아홉	⇨	아홉 개
열	⇨	열 개

Let's Study!

> **Final Consonants 'ㅍ, ㅌ, ㅊ, ㅋ, ㅆ, ㄲ'**

Listen Listen and pay attention to the colored final consonants of the following words. Choose the pronunciation of the final consonant. ▶ track **199**

(1) 잎   (2) 끝   (3) 낮   (4) 밖

Learn When the consonants 'ㅍ, ㅌ, ㅊ, ㅋ, ㅆ, ㄲ' are written as final consonants, they do not maintain their original sounds. Instead, they are pronounced as basic consonants in the same positions.

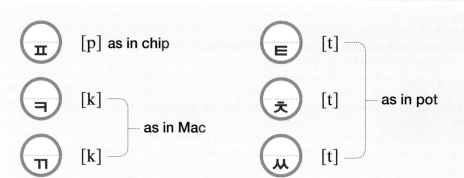

Seven representative final consonant sounds

For the most part, consonants that are written as the initial sound of a syllable can also be final consonants; however, the pronunciation of final consonants is restricted to the following seven sounds [ㅁ, ㄴ, ㄹ, ㅇ, ㅂ, ㄷ, ㄱ]. When the other consonants (ex. ㅍ) are written as final consonants, their pronunciations change to one of these seven representative sounds (ex. ㅍ→[ㅂ]) that is pronounced in the same position.

[m] [n] [l] [ng] [p] [t] [k]

Practice Listen to the following examples and note the difference. ▶ track **200**

❶ When a consonant is the first sound

아 ➡ 파
[a]   [pa]

❷ When a consonant is the final sound of a syllable (*batchim*)

아 ➡ 앞
[a]   [ap]

Pronunciation **Tip**

When pronouncing the sound of a final consonant, to avoid pronouncing a syllable with a *batchim* as two syllables, be sure to pronounce the vowel quickly.

Ex.

Pronounce it quickly! Make it one syllable!

Practice Let's add a consonant under a vowel. Listen and repeat the audio. ▶ track **201**

❶ 아 ➡ 앞 = 압
[a]   [ap]   [ap]

❷ 아 ➡ 악 = 악
[a]   [ak]   [ak]

❸ 아 ➡ 윽 = 악
[a]   [ak]   [ak]

✱ Pronunciation Point

The final consonants 'ㅂ, ㅍ' are pronounced as [ㅂ], 'ㄱ, ㅋ, ㄲ' are pronounced as [ㄱ], and 'ㄷ, ㅌ, ㅅ, ㅆ, ㅈ, ㅊ, ㅎ' are pronounced as [ㄷ]. These final consonants have the same sound but different meanings.
▶ track **202**

(1)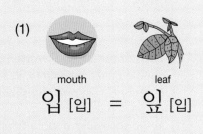

mouth   leaf

입 [입] = 잎 [입]

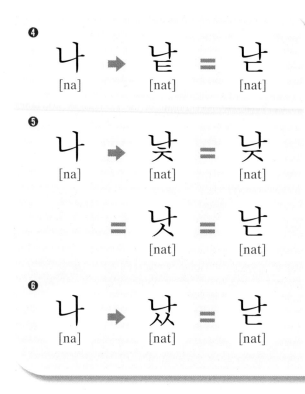

❹ 나 [na] ➜ 낱 [nat] = 낟 [nat]

❺ 나 [na] ➜ 낯 [nat] = 낯 [nat]

= 낫 [nat] = 낟 [nat]

❻ 나 [na] ➜ 났 [nat] = 낟 [nat]

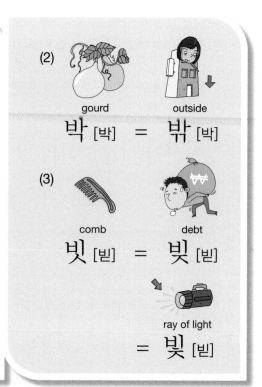

(2)
gourd   outside
박 [박] = 밖 [박]

(3)
comb   debt
빗 [빋] = 빚 [빋]

ray of light
= 빛 [빋]

▸ **Double Final Consonants**

Listen Listen and pay attention to the colored double final consonants of the following words. Choose the pronunciation of the double final consonants. ▸ track **203**

ㄱ ㅁ ㅂ

(1) 값 (2) 몫 (3) 닭 (4) 삶

Learn Two consonants are written together as double final consonants. When pronouncing double final consonants, in some cases, only the first consonant is pronounced while in other cases, only the second consonant is pronounced. ▸ track **204**

(1) In the following double final consonants (ㄵ, ㄶ, ㄼ, ㄽ, ㅀ, ㅄ, ㄳ, etc.) only the first consonant is pronounced.

앉다 많고 여덟 핥다 옳지 없다 삯

(2) In the following double final consonants (ㄺ, ㄻ, etc.) only the second consonant is pronounced.

흙 까닭 앎 삶

Reading Activity!

1 Read the following. Listen and repeat the audio. ▶track **205**

(1) 앞 옆 짚 숲

(2) 끝 팥 낱 홑

(3) 밑 빛 꽃 숯

(4) 억 녁

(5) 었 갔 섰 했

(6) 밖 닦 낚 솎

(7) 몫 삯

(8) 값 없

(9) 닭 칡

(10) 앎 삶

2 Listen and mark O if correct or X if incorrect. ▶track **206**

(1) 솥 ( )

(2) 윷 ( )

(3) 밖 ( )

(4) 흙 ( )

(5) 값 ( )

(6) 꽃 ( )

(7) 옆 ( )

(8) 삶 ( )

(9) 밑 ( )

(10) 몇 ( )

3 Choose the correct answer that has a completely different pronunciation from the other two. Check the answer by listening to the audio. ▶track **207**

(1) ⓐ 꼭 ⓑ 꽂 ⓒ 꽃

(2) ⓐ 숩 ⓑ 숨 ⓒ 숲

(3) ⓐ 낙 ⓑ 낚 ⓒ 났

(4) ⓐ 숯 ⓑ 숫 ⓒ 숙

4 Listen and choose the correct answer. ▶track **208**

(1) ⓐ 겉 ☐　ⓑ 겁 ☐　　　(2) ⓐ 갚다 ☐　ⓑ 같다 ☐

(3) ⓐ 몇 ☐　ⓑ 멱 ☐　　　(4) ⓐ 났어요 ☐　ⓑ 낚아요 ☐

(5) ⓐ 달 ☐　ⓑ 닭 ☐　　　(6) ⓐ 했어요 ☐　ⓑ 해서요 ☐

(7) ⓐ 못 ☐　ⓑ 몿 ☐　　　(8) ⓐ 않아요 ☐　ⓑ 앉아요 ☐

5 Listen and number the words in order. ▶track **209**

부엌 ☐　　여덟 ☐　　눈빛 ☐　　있어요 ☐

까닭 ☐　　꽃병 ☐　　돌솥 ☐　　닭고기 ☐

바깥 ☐　　무릎 ☐　　숯불 ☐　　갔어요 ☐

6 Listen and match the picture with the word. ▶track **210**

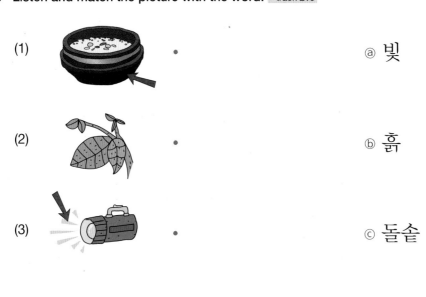

(1)　　　•　　　　　　　　ⓐ 빛

(2)　　　•　　　　　　　　ⓑ 흙

(3)　　　•　　　　　　　　ⓒ 돌솥

(4)　　　•　　　　　　　　ⓓ 잎

★ Special Pronunciation Rule

Learn The rules of final consonant pronunciation are as follows.

1 The pronunciation of the final consonants differs when used alone and followed by a vowel.

When used alone as a final consonant, the pronunciations of the consonants 'ㅍ, ㅋ, ㄲ, ㅌ, ㅊ, ㅆ' are as follows: 'ㅍ' → [ㅂ]; 'ㅋ, ㄲ' → [ㄱ]; and 'ㅌ, ㅊ, ㅆ' → [ㄷ]. On the other hand, when a final consonant is followed by a vowel, it maintains its original sound and is pronounced as the initial sound of the following syllable. ▶track 211

Ex. (1) 앞 [압]　앞이 [아피]　(2) 밖 [박]　밖에 [바께]

(3) 꽃 [꼳]　꽃이 [꼬치]　(4) 빛 [빋]　빛을 [비츨]

2 The pronunciation of the final consonants differs when used alone and followed by a vowel.

When a double final consonant is used alone as a syllable, the pronunciation of the double final consonant takes on either the sound of the first or second consonant (ex. 값[갑]) according to the rule. On the other hand, when followed by a vowel, the first consonant of the double final consonant is pronounced, and the second consonant maintains its original sound and is pronounced as the initial sound of the following syllable (ex. 값을[갑슬]). ▶track 212

Ex. (1) 닭 [닥]　닭이 [달기]　(2) 값 [갑]　값을 [갑슬]

(3) 삶 [삼]　삶에 [살메]　(4) 삯 [삭]　삯을 [삭슬]

3 The 'ㅎ' in double final consonants is dropped when followed by a vowel.

When the second consonant of a double final consonant is 'ㅎ' (ㄶ, ㅀ), and is followed by a vowel, the first consonant of the double final consonant is pronounced as [ㄴ, ㄹ] and the second consonant's sound [ㅎ] is dropped. ▶track 213

Ex. (1) 많이 [마니]　(2) 않아요 [아나요]

(3) 싫어요 [시러요]　(4) 잃어요 [이러요]

Practice Listen and number the words in order. ▶track 214

옆집 □	읽은 □	꽃을 □	무릎에 □
몇 살 □	많이 □	볶음 □	싫어요 □
밑줄 □	젊음 □	끝에 □	없어요 □

Writing Activity!

The position for writing final consonants

▸ As the final sound of a syllable, final consonants are written at the bottom (within a single square). In the case of double final consonants, the position for final consonants is shared, and the two final consonants are written from left to right.

1 Listen and repeat the following syllables after the audio. Write them in the correct stroke order. ▸ track **215**

(1)			(2)			(3)		
앞	앞	앞	꽃	꽃	꽃	닭	닭	닭
숲	숲	숲	낮	낮	낮	삶	삶	삶
짚	짚	짚	빛	빛	빛	값	값	값
끝	끝	끝	억	억	억	몫	몫	몫
밭	밭	밭	밖	밖	밖	앉	앉	앉
팥	팥	팥	있	있	있	않	않	않

2 Listen and write the word. ▶track **216**

끝
end

숲
forest

무릎
knee

꽃
flower

부엌
kitchen

밖
outside

닭
chicken

값
price

1 Choose the correct answer that has a completely different pronunciation from the other two. Check the answer by listening to the audio. ▶track 217

(1) ⓐ 마이　　ⓑ 마니　　ⓒ 많이

(2) ⓐ 안자서　　ⓑ 앉아서　　ⓒ 안아서

(3) ⓐ 일어요　　ⓑ 일러요　　ⓒ 잃어요

(4) ⓐ 다가요　　ⓑ 다까요　　ⓒ 닦아요

2 Listen and number the words in order. ▶track 218

3 Listen and follow the path of the words you hear. Write the letter you arrive at. ▶ track **219**

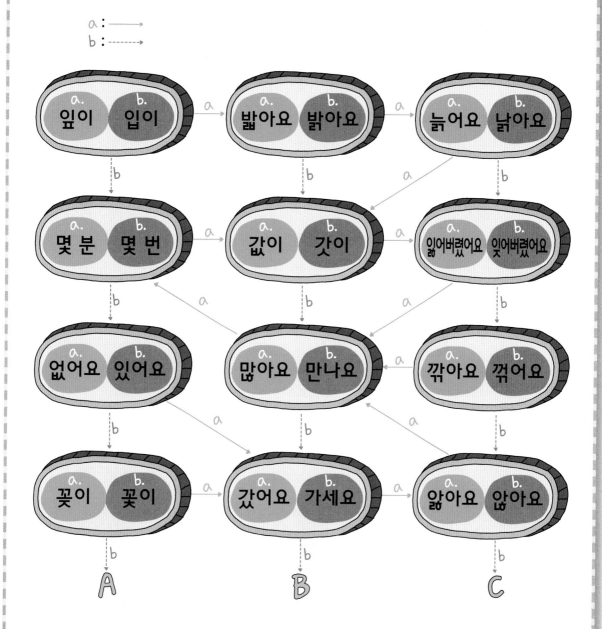

Final Answer: _____

4 Listen and write the letter that matches the picture. ▶track **220**

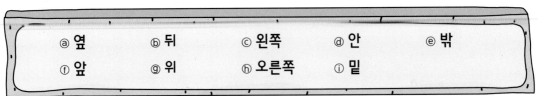

ⓐ 옆 ⓑ 뒤 ⓒ 왼쪽 ⓓ 안 ⓔ 밖
ⓕ 앞 ⓖ 위 ⓗ 오른쪽 ⓘ 밑

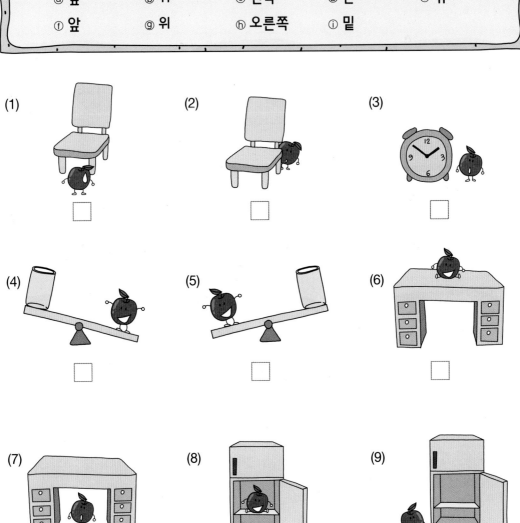

(1)

(2)

(3)

(4)

(5)

(6)

(7)

(8)

(9)

5 Look at the pictures. Listen and complete the word. ▶track **221**

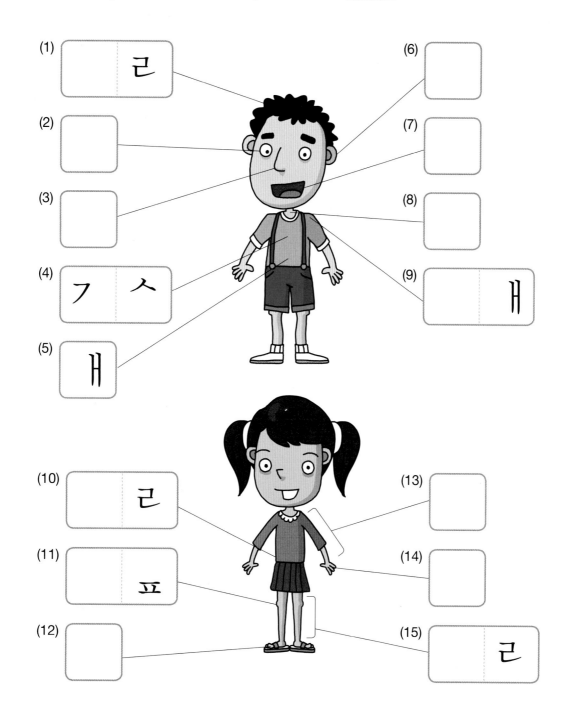

(1) 　ㄹ

(2)

(3)

(4) ㄱ　ㅅ

(5) ㅐ

(6)

(7)

(8)

(9) 　ㅐ

(10) 　ㄹ

(11) 　ㅍ

(12)

(13)

(14)

(15) 　ㄹ

Final Review

Nineteen consonants

Depending on the strength of the air	• Basic consonants (Pronounce by not using much air) • Aspirated consonants (Pronounce by using a lot of air) • Tensed consonants (Pronounce stronger with a tight throat, not using much air)

The method of pronunciation	The position of pronunciation	Bilabial sound (Pronounce by using the lips)		Alveolar sound (Pronounce by touching the end of the tongue behind the upper teeth)	
Plosive (Pronounce by puffing strong air)	Basic consonants	ㅂ	[b] table [p] pop	ㄷ	[d] studio [t] bet
	Aspirated consonants	ㅍ	[p] peace	ㅌ	[t] teacher
	Tensed consonants	ㅃ	[pp] bad!	ㄸ	[tt] duh! (Strong pronunciation)
Fricative (Pronounce with friction via a narrowed articulator organ)	Basic consonants			ㅅ	[s] sky [sh] she (Before 'ㅣ, ㅑ, ㅕ, ㅛ, ㅠ')
	Tensed consonants			ㅆ	[ss] sang
Affricate (Pronounce by puffing air with friction)	Basic consonants				
	Aspirated consonants				
	Tensed consonants				
Nasal (Pronounce by using the nose)		ㅁ	[m] money, moon	ㄴ	[n] no, now
Liquid [r] (Pronounce by touching the end of the tongue behind the upper teeth) [ℓ] (Pronounce by placing the tip of the tongue on the upper gum and let the air flow from side to side)				ㄹ	[r] X-ray [ℓ] lollipop

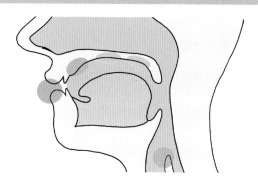

Palatal sound (Pronounce by touching the tongue along the front palate)		Velar sound (Pronounce by touching the tongue on the back of the palate)		Glottal sound (Pronounce with the larynx)	
		ㄱ	[g] baggage [k] pick		
		ㅋ	[k] kitchen		
		ㄲ	[kk] gotcha!		
				ㅎ	[h] him
ㅈ	[j] juice [ch] church				
ㅊ	[ch] chicken				
ㅉ	[jj] gotcha!				
		ㅇ	[ng] song (Only final consonants)		

Twenty-one vowels

Basic vowels	[y] vowels	Basic vowels	[y] vowels
ㅏ [a] father	ㅑ [ya] yard	ㅓ [eo] honest	ㅕ [yeo] yawn
ㅗ [o] nobody, hola	ㅛ [yo] yoga	ㅜ [u] who	ㅠ [yu] you
ㅡ [eu] taken		ㅣ [i] bee, teeth	
ㅐ [ae] cat, pat	ㅒ [yae] yak, yap	ㅔ [e] end, pen	ㅖ [ye] yes, yet

[w] vowels		The other vowel
ㅘ [wa] wine	ㅝ [weo] walk	
ㅙ [wae] wag	ㅞ [we] wedding	ㅢ [ui] gooey
ㅚ [oe] weight	ㅟ [wi] we	

Appendix I

- Answers
- Listening Scripts
- Index

Answers

Chapter 1

STEP 1 Let's Warm Up!

2 (1) 1   (2) 4   (3) 8   (4) 6

3 (1) 2   (2) 5   (3) 7   (4) 9

STEP 2 Let's Study!

*Pronunciation Point

2 (1) ⓑ   (2) ⓑ   (3) ⓐ   (4) ⓐ

STEP 3 Reading Activity!

2 (1) ⓑ → ⓒ → ⓕ → ⓐ → ⓔ → ⓓ
    (2) ⓕ → ⓒ → ⓑ → ⓓ → ⓐ → ⓔ

3
아 ④	이 ⑥	아이 ⑤	아우 ③
오 ①	어이 ⑦	오이 ②	우이 ⑧

4 (1) ⓒ   (2) ⓐ   (3) ⓓ   (4) ⓑ

STEP 4 Writing Activity!

2 (1) 아   (2) 우   (3) 어   (4) 으
   (5) 오 이   (6) 아 이
   (7) 아 우   (8) 이

STEP 5 Quiz Yourself!

1 (1) ×   (2) ○   (3) ×   (4) ○

2
⑤ 이	⑦ 오이	③ 아우
⑧ 우	⑨ 아이	① 오
② 아	④ 어이	⑥ 우이

3 (1) 아 이   (2) 오 이
   (3) 아 우   (4) 어 이

Chapter 2

STEP 1 Let's Warm Up!

2 (1) ⓓ   (2) ⓑ   (3) ⓔ   (4) ⓐ   (5) ⓒ

STEP 3 Reading Activity!

2 (1) ○   (2) ×   (3) ×   (4) ○

3 (1) ⓑ   (2) ⓐ   (3) ⓐ   (4) ⓑ   (5) ⓑ   (6) ⓐ

4
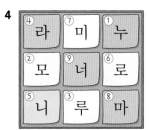
④ 라	⑦ 미	① 누
② 모	⑨ 너	⑥ 로
⑤ 니	③ 루	⑧ 마

5
이미 ⑤	이마 ①	나라 ⑪	누나 ④
어미 ⑧	머리 ⑥	모이 ②	머루 ⑨
나무 ③	너무 ⑩	우리 ⑦	노루 ⑫

6 (1) 모   (2) 너   (3) 리   (4) 미

7 (1) ⓒ   (2) ⓐ   (3) ⓓ   (4) ⓑ

STEP 4 Writing Activity!

2 (1) 모   (2) 미   (3) 너   (4) 누   (5) 리
   (6) 어, 머   (7) 라   (8) 마, 리

3 (1) ① 우   (2) ② 마   (3) ① 너   (4) ① 머   (5) ② 라

STEP 5 Quiz Yourself!

Chapter 3

STEP 1 Let's Warm Up!

2 (1) ⓔ (2) ⓐ (3) ⓒ (4) ⓑ (5) ⓓ

STEP 3 Reading Activity!

2 (1) × (2) ○ (3) × (4) ○ (5) ×
(6) ○ (7) × (8) × (9) ○ (10) ×

3 (1) ⓐ (2) ⓑ (3) ⓑ (4) ⓑ (5) ⓐ
(6) ⓑ (7) ⓑ (8) ⓑ (9) ⓐ

4

바지 9	기자 4	지하 7	드라마 2
가로 3	두부 11	고사 10	아버지 8
무시 6	후기 1	자비 12	도자기 5

5 (1) 서 (2) 다 (3) 두 (4) 구 (5) 버
(6) 지 (7) 시 (8) 주 (9) 후 (10) 도

6 (1) ⓓ (2) ⓐ (3) ⓑ (4) ⓒ

7

⑩ 거리	③ 허리	⑧ 바다	⑤ 사자
⑬ 바로	⑥ 구이	⑮ 기사	② 우주
① 하나	⑯ 자리	⑪ 지하	⑦ 오후
⑨ 조사	⑭ 도시	④ 가수	⑫ 모기

STEP 4 Writing Activity!

2 (1) 구 (2) 시 (3) 기 (4) 수 (5) 두 (6) 리, 고
(7) 보 (8) 버, 지 (9) 하 (10) 비, 스

STEP 5 Quiz Yourself!

1 (1) ⓐ 조리 ☑ ⓑ 저리 □ (2) ⓐ 바지 ☑ ⓑ 비자 □
(3) ⓐ 고리 □ ⓑ 거리 ☑ (4) ⓐ 조사 □ ⓑ 주사 ☑
(5) ⓐ 수다 ☑ ⓑ 다수 □ (6) ⓐ 나리 □ ⓑ 다리 ☑
(7) ⓐ 서기 ☑ ⓑ 사기 □ (8) ⓐ 소수 □ ⓑ 조수 ☑

2

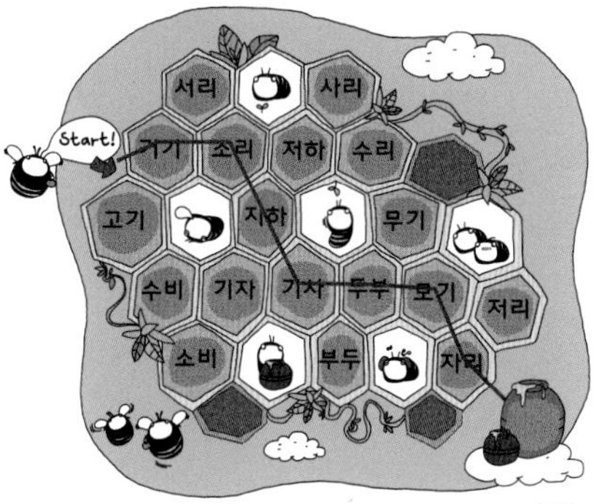

Final Answer: 자리

Chapter 4

STEP 1 Let's Warm Up!

2 (1) ⓔ (2) ⓐ (3) ⓖ (4) ⓓ (5) ⓑ (6) ⓕ

STEP 2 Let's Study!

Listen (1) ㅂ (2) ㄹ (3) ㅁ (4) ㄱ

STEP 3 Reading Activity!

2 (1) ○ (2) × (3) × (4) ○ (5) ×
(6) × (7) ○ (8) × (9) ○ (10) ×

3 (1) ⓑ (2) ⓐ (3) ⓐ (4) ⓐ (5) ⓐ
(6) ⓑ (7) ⓑ (8) ⓑ (9) ⓐ

4

아들 3	도장 9	이름 1	아줌마 6
한국 11	음식 4	거울 10	밀가루 12
시간 2	남산 7	수업 5	젓가락 8

5 (1) 람 (2) 국 (3) 진 (4) 곱 (5) 장 (6) 섯

6 (1) ⓓ (2) ⓐ (3) ⓒ (4) ⓑ

7 (1) ⓑ (2) ⓐ (3) ⓐ (4) ⓑ (5) ⓐ (6) ⓑ

*Special Pronunciation Rule

1

발음 8	얼음 12	웃음 5	녹음 3
만일 4	단어 1	언어 9	본인 7
직업 10	믿음 6	금일 2	길이 11

2 (1) 발 (2) 음 (3) 단 (4) 업
(5) 음 (6) 음 (7) 종 (8) 인

STEP 4 Writing Activity!

2 (1) 름 (2) 작 (3) 부, 님
(4) 불 (5) 랑 (6) 아, 줌

STEP 5 Quiz Yourself!

1 (1) ⓐ 삼 □ ⓑ 섬 ☑ ⓒ 솜 □ ⓓ 숨 □
(2) ⓐ 반 □ ⓑ 번 □ ⓒ 본 □ ⓓ 분 ☑
(3) ⓐ 성 ☑ ⓑ 선 □ ⓒ 섬 □ ⓓ 설 □
(4) ⓐ 공 □ ⓑ 곤 □ ⓒ 곰 □ ⓓ 골 ☑

2

⑨ 직업	④ 곧	② 바람
① 혼자	⑥ 명	⑧ 빛
⑦ 동물	장난	⑤ 식당

3

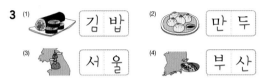

(1) 김 밥   (2) 만 두

(3) 서 울   (4) 부 산

4

5

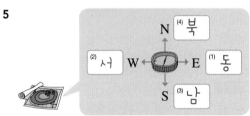

N ⁽⁴⁾북
⁽²⁾서 W E ⁽¹⁾동
S ⁽³⁾남

6

⁽⁷⁾하 늘
⁽¹⁰⁾눈 ⁽¹⁾산 ⁽⁹⁾비
⁽⁸⁾바 람
⁽²⁾나 무 ⁽³⁾강 ⁽⁴⁾절 ⁽⁵⁾바 다 ⁽⁶⁾섬

Chapter 5

STEP 1 Let's Warm Up!

2 (1) ⓒ (2) ⓗ (3) ⓘ (4) ⓔ (5) ⓖ

STEP 2 Let's Study!

*Pronunciation Point

2 (1) ⓐ (2) ⓑ (3) ⓑ (4) ⓑ

STEP 3 Reading Activity!

2 (1) × (2) ○ (3) ○ (4) ○ (5) ×

3 (1) ⓑ (2) ⓐ (3) ⓐ (4) ⓑ
　(5) ⓑ (6) ⓐ (7) ⓐ (8) ⓑ

4

② 무료	⑧ 경기	⑤ 공연
⑥ 현금	① 서양	⑨ 연구
④ 학교	⑦ 노력	③ 기념

5

우유 ⑪	중요 ⑦	여자 ⑤	수요일 ③
여유 ④	여름 ⑩	양말 ①	일요일 ⑫
무역 ⑧	안경 ②	영어 ⑨	주유소 ⑥

6 (1) 야 (2) 유 (3) 영 (4) 겨
　(5) 료 (6) 명 (7) 연 (8) 녕

7 (1) ⓒ (2) ⓓ (3) ⓐ (4) ⓑ

*Special Pronunciation Rule

STEP 4 Writing Activity!

2 (1) 여 (2) 용 (3) 아, 요 (4) 유 (5) 양
(6) 며, 리 (7) 연 (8) 녁 (9) 영, 중

STEP 5 Quiz Yourself!

1

①수	염		②여	가		⑤야
수			드		⑥안	경
료		③여	름		녕	
		자		⑦주		
	④고		⑥자	유		
④서	양	인		⑦소	⑧유	
	이				⑧명	동

2

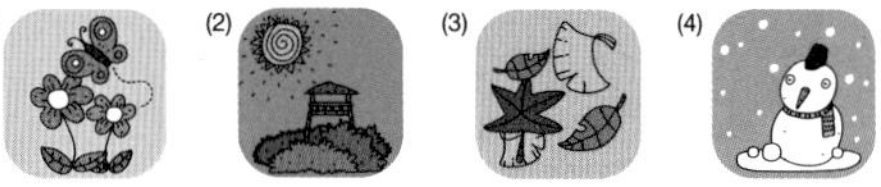

(1) 봄 (2) 여름 (3) 가을 (4) 겨울

3

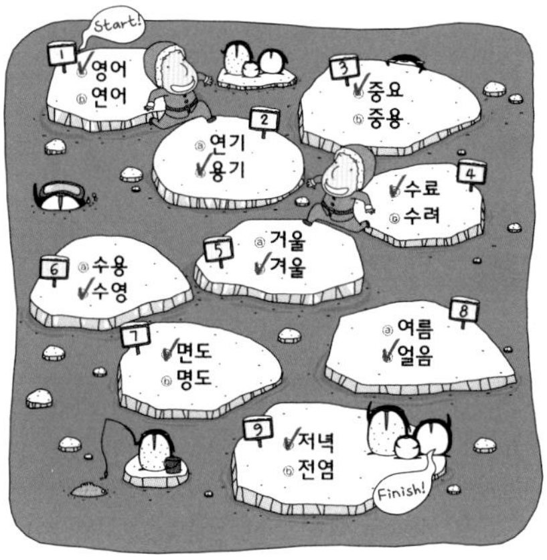

Chapter 6

STEP 1 Let's Warm Up!

2 (1) ⓒ (2) ⓐ (3) ⓔ (4) ⓑ (5) ⓓ

STEP 3 Reading Activity!

2 (1) ○ (2) × (3) ○ (4) ×
(5) ○ (6) ○ (7) × (8) ×

3 (1) ⓑ (2) ⓐ (3) ⓐ (4) ⓑ
(5) ⓐ (6) ⓑ (7) ⓑ (8) ⓐ

4

내일 7	숙제 5	인생 10	남동생 3
문제 2	세상 12	가게 8	제주도 11
얘기 9	계속 4	예약 1	냉장고 6

5 (1) 내 (2) 대 (3) 개 (4) 세
(5) 레 (6) 생 (7) 예 (8) 개

6 (1) ⓓ (2) ⓑ (3) ⓐ (4) ⓒ

7

10 생일	12 세계	4 소개	7 매일
3 기대	1 재미	9 경제	5 오래
11 반대	6 예상	8 계절	2 생각

*Special Pronunciation Rule

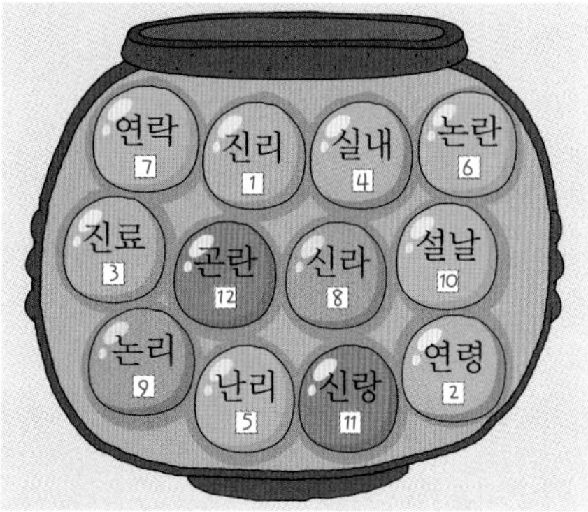

STEP 5 Quiz Yourself!

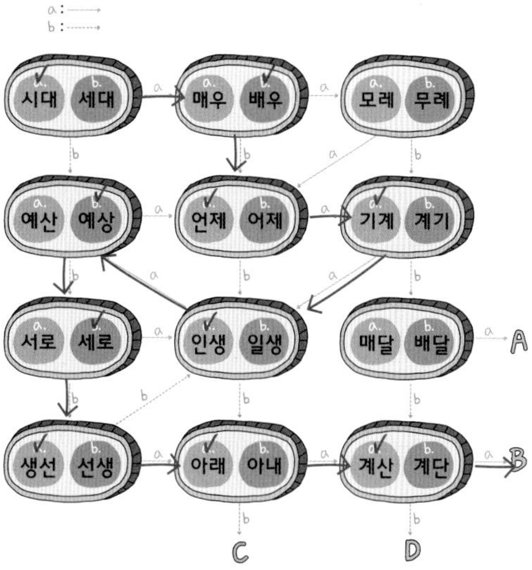

Final Answer: B

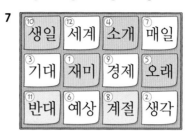

Chapter 7

STEP 1 **Let's Warm Up!**

2 (1) ⓕ   (2) ⓓ   (3) ⓑ   (4) ⓔ   (5) ⓒ

STEP 3 **Reading Activity!**

2 (1) ○   (2) ✕   (3) ○   (4) ✕   (5) ○
　 (6) ○   (7) ○   (8) ✕   (9) ○   (10) ✕

3 (1) ⓑ   (2) ⓑ   (3) ⓐ   (4) ⓑ
　 (5) ⓐ   (6) ⓑ   (7) ⓑ   (8) ⓐ

4

김치 ④	크기 ①	선택 ⑦	지하철 ⑨
통역 ⑩	부탁 ⑫	봉투 ②	스포츠 ⑤
추석 ⑧	경치 ⑥	출구 ⑪	자동차 ③

5 (1) 터   (2) 카   (3) 파   (4) 토
　 (5) 표   (6) 체   (7) 친   (8) 통

6 (1) ⓑ   (2) ⓒ   (3) ⓐ   (4) ⓓ

***Special Pronunciation Rule**

1

입학 ②	놓다 ⑤	육 호선 ⑦	이렇게 ④
맏형 ⑥	좋고 ①	못해요 ③	그렇지 ⑧

2 (1) 습   (2) 각   (3) 복   (4) 슷

STEP 4 **Writing Activity!**

2 (1) 포   (2) 통   (3) 치   (4) 편   (5) 출
　 (6) 착   (7) 필   (8) 갈, 탕   (9) 친   (10) 컴, 터

STEP 5 **Quiz Yourself!**

1

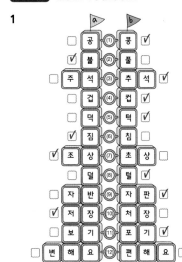

2

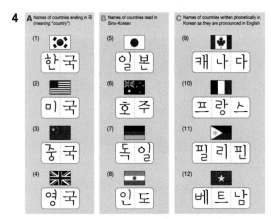

3

4

A Names of countries ending in 국 (meaning "country")	B Names of countries read in Sino-Korean	C Names of countries written phonetically in Korean as they are pronounced in English
(1) 한국	(5) 일본	(9) 캐나다
(2) 미국	(6) 호주	(10) 프랑스
(3) 중국	(7) 독일	(11) 필리핀
(4) 영국	(8) 인도	(12) 베트남

5 (1) 명동   (2) 남산   (3) 시청   (4) 홍대
　 (5) 남대문 시장   (6) 동대문 시장
　 (7) 경복궁   (8) 광화문   (9) 강남역
　 (10) 서울역   (11) 이태원   (12) 종로

Chapter 8

STEP 1 **Let's Warm Up!**

2 (1) ⓒ   (2) ⓔ   (3) ⓐ   (4) ⓓ   (5) ⓖ   (6) ⓕ

STEP 2 Let's Study!

*Pronunciation Point

2 (1) ⓑ (2) ⓒ (3) ⓐ (4) ⓑ

STEP 3 Reading Activity!

2 (1) ○ (2) × (3) × (4) ○ (5) ×
(6) ○ (7) × (8) ○ (9) × (10) ○

3 (1) ⓐ (2) ⓑ (3) ⓑ (4) ⓑ (5) ⓑ
(6) ⓐ (7) ⓐ (8) ⓑ (9) ⓐ (10) ⓐ

4

위험 ④	취소 ⑪	교회 ⑧	추워요 ②
병원 ⑦	의견 ③	영화 ⑤	대사관 ⑩
희망 ⑨	최고 ⑫	과일 ①	매워요 ⑥

5 (1) 과 (2) 화 (3) 회 (4) 워 (5) 의
(6) 좌 (7) 돼 (8) 외 (9) 훼 (10) 휘

6 (1) ⓒ (2) ⓐ (3) ⓓ (4) ⓑ

*Special Pronunciation Rule

STEP 4 Writing Activity!

2 (1) 화 (2) 의 (3) 교 (4) 위 (5) 지 (6) 송
(7) 망 (8) 국 (9) 관 (10) 원 (11) 위 (12) 쉬

3 (1) 과 (2) 위 (3) 의 (4) 취 (5) 화 (6) 워

STEP 5 Quiz Yourself!

1

2
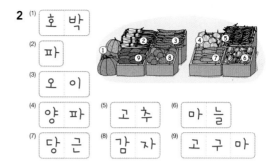

(1) 호 박 (2) 파 (3) 오 이 (4) 양 파 (5) 고 추 (6) 마 늘 (7) 당 근 (8) 감 자 (9) 고 구 마

3
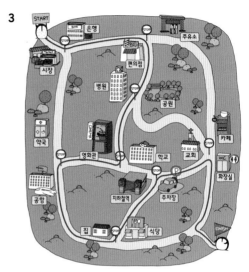

4

Answers · **159**

Chapter 9

STEP 1 Let's Warm Up!

2 (1) ⓒ (2) ⓙ (3) ⓑ (4) ⓐ (5) ⓕ

STEP 3 Reading Activity!

2 (1) ○ (2) × (3) ○ (4) × (5) ×
(6) ○ (7) × (8) × (9) ○ (10) ○

3 (1) ⓐ (2) ⓑ (3) ⓑ (4) ⓐ
(5) ⓐ (6) ⓑ (7) ⓑ (8) ⓐ

4

떡 ⑥	뿌리 ⑧	씨름 ⑫	아저씨 ⑨
짝 ⑩	가끔 ③	토끼 ①	깨끗이 ④
빵 ②	눈썹 ⑤	뚜껑 ⑪	어쩐지 ⑦

5 (1) 짜 (2) 따 (3) 빨 (4) 끼 (5) 낌
(6) 쪽 (7) 찌 (8) 빠 (9) 싸 (10) 까

6 (1) ⓑ (2) ⓓ (3) ⓒ (4) ⓐ

*Special Pronunciation Rule

1

목적 ⑤	늦게 ⑩	혹시 ①	숟가락 ⑫
역시 ⑧	습관 ⑪	집중 ⑦	갑자기 ③
옷장 ②	덕분 ④	각각 ⑨	목소리 ⑥

2

(1) 약속 appointment
(2) 책상 desk
(3) 듣기 listening
(4) 입구 entrance
(5) 박수 clapping
(6) 낮잠 nap

STEP 4 Writing Activity!

2 (1) 꾸 (2) 씨 (3) 빨 (4) 짜 (5) 깐
(6) 싸 (7) 짝 (8) 씨 (9) 씀 (10) 뻐

STEP 5 Quiz Yourself!

1

2

⑰빵집	④글쎄	⑭똑바로	②쯤	⑥일찍
⑨벌써	⑮짜증	㉑쑥	⑫따로	⑳꼭지
⑬싸움	⑩나빠요	⑦함께	⑤손뼉	㉔예뻐요
㉕팔꿈치	⑲뿌리	①쓰기	⑯꾸중	⑪그때
③진짜	㉓깜짝	⑱짜리	⑦살짝	⑧또

3

(1) 사과 (2) 배
(3) 딸기 (4) 포도
(5) 수박 (6) 바나나
(7) 감 (8) 귤

Chapter 10

STEP 1 Let's Warm Up!

1 (1) ⓔ (2) ⓐ (3) ⓓ (4) ⓒ (5) ⓙ
(6) ① (7) ⓖ (8) ⓕ (9) ⓗ (10) ⓑ

2 (1) ⓑ (2) ⓒ (3) ⓓ (4) ⓐ

STEP 2 Let's Study!

Listen

Final Consonants ㅍ, ㅌ, ㅊ, ㅋ, ㅆ, ㄲ

(1) ㅂ (2) ㄷ (3) ㄷ (4) ㄱ

Double Final Consonants

(1) ㅂ (2) ㄱ (3) ㄱ (4) ㅁ

2 (1) ○　(2) ✕　(3) ○　(4) ✕　(5) ○
　　(6) ○　(7) ✕　(8) ○　(9) ○　(10) ✕

3 (1) ⓐ　(2) ⓑ　(3) ⓒ　(4) ⓒ

4 (1) ⓐ 겉 ✔　ⓑ 겁 ☐　　(2) ⓐ 갚다 ✔　ⓑ 같다 ☐
　　(3) ⓐ 몇 ✔　ⓑ 멱 ☐　　(4) ⓐ 났어요 ☐　ⓑ 낚아요 ✔
　　(5) ⓐ 달 ☐　ⓑ 닭 ✔　　(6) ⓐ 했어요 ✔　ⓑ 해서요 ☐
　　(7) ⓐ 못 ☐　ⓑ 못 ✔　　(8) ⓐ 앉아요 ✔　ⓑ 않아요 ☐

5

부엌 ⑨	여덟 ①	눈빛 ⑤	있어요 ⑫
까닭 ⑥	꽃병 ⑩	돌솥 ②	닭고기 ⑦
바깥 ④	무릎 ⑧	숯불 ⑪	갔어요 ③

6 (1) ⓒ　(2) ⓓ　(3) ⓐ　(4) ⓑ

*Special Pronunciation Rule

옆집 ⑩	읽은 ⑦	꽃을 ⑤	무릎에 ③
몇 살 ⑧	많이 ①	볶음 ⑪	싫어요 ⑥
밑줄 ④	젊음 ⑨	끝에 ②	없어요 ⑫

1 (1) ✔ 마이　ⓑ 마니　ⓒ 많이
　　(2) ⓐ 안자서　ⓑ 앉아서　✔ 안아서
　　(3) ⓐ 일어요　✔ 일러요　ⓒ 잃어요
　　(4) ✔ 다가요　ⓑ 다까요　ⓒ 닭아요

2

3

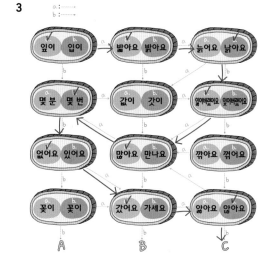

Final Answer: C

4

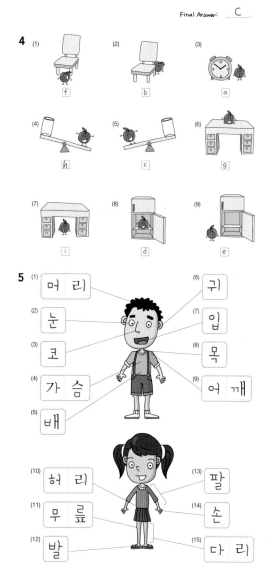

(1) f　(2) b　(3) a
(4) h　(5) c　(6) g
(7) i　(8) d　(9) e

5
(1) 머리　(6) 귀
(2) 눈　(7) 입
(3) 코　(8) 목
(4) 가슴　(9) 어깨
(5) 배

(10) 허리　(13) 팔
(11) 무릎　(14) 손
(12) 발　(15) 다리

Listening Scripts

Chapter 1

STEP 1 Let's Warm Up!

1 ⓐ일　ⓑ이　ⓒ삼　ⓓ사
ⓔ오　ⓕ육　ⓖ칠　ⓗ팔
ⓘ구　ⓙ십

2 (1) 일　(2) 사　(3) 팔　(4) 육

3 (1) 이　(2) 오　(3) 칠　(4) 구

4 (1) 삼일오이
(2) 공일공에 구칠사팔에 육이삼오
(3) 구팔일일이삼에 사구오이삼공

STEP 2 Let's Study!

Listen (1) 이 (2) 오

Learn 아, 어, 오, 우, 으, 이

*Pronunciation Point

1 (1) 오, 어　(2) 우, 으

2 (1) 오　(2) 어　(3) 우　(4) 으

STEP 3 Reading Activity!

1 ⓐ아　ⓑ어　ⓒ오　ⓓ우
ⓔ으　ⓕ이

2 (1) 어, 오, 이, 아, 으, 우
(2) 이, 오, 어, 우, 아, 으

3 (1) 오　(2) 오이　(3) 아우　(4) 아
(5) 아이　(6) 이　(7) 어이　(8) 우이

4 (1) 이　(2) 오　(3) 오이　(4) 아이

STEP 4 Writing Activity!

1 아, 어, 오, 우, 으, 이

2 (1) 아　(2) 우　(3) 어　(4) 으
(5) 오이　(6) 아이　(7) 아우　(8) 이

3 이, 오, 아이, 오이, 이, 아, 아우, 우이

STEP 5 Quiz Yourself!

1 (1) 어　(2) 오　(3) 우　(4) 어

2 (1) 오　(2) 아　(3) 아우　(4) 어이
(5) 이　(6) 우이　(7) 오이　(8) 우
(9) 아이

3 (1) 아이　(2) 오이　(3) 아우　(4) 어이

Chapter 2

STEP 1 Let's Warm Up!

1 ⓐ김밥　ⓑ라면　ⓒ만두　ⓓ비빔밥
ⓔ불고기 ⓕ찌개

2 (1) 비빔밥 (2) 라면　(3) 불고기　(4) 김밥
(5) 만두

3 Ex.1 A: 김밥이에요?　B: 네.
Ex.2 A: 김밥이에요?　B: 아니요.
(1) A: 라면이에요?　B: 네.
(2) A: 만두예요?　B: 아니요.
(3) A: 찌개예요?　B: 아니요.
(4) A: 비빔밥이에요?　B: 네.

STEP 2 Let's Study!

Listen (1) 만두　(2) 네　(3) 라면

Practice
(1) 아, 마 (2) 아, 나　(3) 아, 라　(4) 오, 모
(5) 오, 노 (6) 오, 로　(7) 이, 미　(8) 이, 니
(9) 이, 리

*Pronunciation Point

(1) 라라　(2) 루루　(3) 리리

STEP 3 Reading Activity!

1 (1) 아, 어, 오, 우, 으, 이
(2) 마, 머, 모, 무, 므, 미
(3) 나, 너, 노, 누, 느, 니
(4) 라, 러, 로, 루, 르, 리

2 (1) 머 　(2) 너 　(3) 라 　(4) 무

3 (1) 리 　(2) 너 　(3) 느 　(4) 무
　(5) 노 　(6) 머

4 (1) 누 　(2) 모 　(3) 루 　(4) 라
　(5) 니 　(6) 로 　(7) 미 　(8) 마
　(9) 너

5 (1) 이마 　(2) 모이 　(3) 나무 　(4) 누나
　(5) 이미 　(6) 머리 　(7) 우리 　(8) 어미
　(9) 머루 　(10) 너무 　(11) 나라 　(12) 노루

6 (1) 모이 　(2) 너무 　(3) 나리 　(4) 미리

7 (1) 머리 　(2) 이마 　(3) 어머니 　(4) 나무

STEP 4 Writing Activity!

1 (1) 마, 머, 모, 무, 므, 미
　(2) 나, 너, 노, 누, 느, 니
　(3) 라, 러, 로, 루, 르, 리

2 (1) 이모 　(2) 이미 　(3) 너무 　(4) 누나
　(5) 우리 　(6) 어머니 　(7) 나라 　(8) 마무리

3 Ex. 누이 　(1) 우리 　(2) 이마 　(3) 너무
　(4) 머리 　(5) 나라

4 나이, 나무, 이마, 오리, 어머니, 머리,
　누나, 나라

STEP 5 Quiz Yourself!

1 (1) 아마 　(2) 노루 　(3) 미모 　(4) 마리
　(5) 우리 　(6) 어미 　(7) 마루 　(8) 나라

Chapter 3

STEP 1 Let's Warm Up!

1 ⓐ서울 　ⓑ경주 　ⓒ부산 　ⓓ대전
　ⓔ제주도

2 (1) 제주도 (2) 서울 　(3) 부산 　(4) 경주
　(5) 대전

3 Ex. A: 어디예요? 　　B: 서울이에요.
　(1) A: 어디예요? 　　B: 제주도예요.
　(2) A: 어디예요? 　　B: 부산이에요.
　(3) A: 어디예요? 　　B: 경주예요.

STEP 2 Let's Study!

Listen (1) 부산 　(2) 대전 　(3) 제주도
　　　(4) 경주 　(5) 서울 　(6) 한국

Practice

　(1) 아, 바 　(2) 아, 다 　(3) 아, 사 　(4) 아, 자
　(5) 아, 가 　(6) 아, 하

*Pronunciation Point

1 (1) 부부 　(2) 도도 　(3) 주주 　(4) 기기

2 사시, 스시

STEP 3 Reading Activity!

1 (1) 바, 버, 보, 부, 브, 비
　(2) 다, 더, 도, 두, 드, 디
　(3) 사, 서, 소, 수, 스, 시
　(4) 자, 저, 조, 주, 즈, 지
　(5) 가, 거, 고, 구, 그, 기
　(6) 하, 허, 호, 후, 흐, 히

2 (1) 부 　(2) 서 　(3) 저 　(4) 그
　(5) 바 　(6) 더 　(7) 주 　(8) 거
　(9) 시 　(10) 호

3 (1) 거 　(2) 디 　(3) 주 　(4) 바
　(5) 더 　(6) 구 　(7) 보 　(8) 시
　(9) 허

4 (1) 후기 　(2) 드라마 　(3) 가로 　(4) 기자
　(5) 도자기 (6) 무시 　(7) 지하 　(8) 아버지
　(9) 바지 　(10) 고사 　(11) 두부 　(12) 자비

5 (1) 서로 　(2) 사다리 　(3) 모두 　(4) 고구마
　(5) 버스 　(6) 나머지 　(7) 다시 　(8) 주머니
　(9) 오후 　(10) 도무지

6 (1) 아버지 (2) 바지 　(3) 구두 　(4) 모자

7 (1) 하나 　(2) 우주 　(3) 허리 　(4) 가수
　(5) 사자 　(6) 구이 　(7) 오후 　(8) 바다
　(9) 조사 　(10) 거리 　(11) 지하 　(12) 모기
　(13) 바로 　(14) 도시 　(15) 기사 　(16) 자리

STEP 4 Writing Activity!

1 (1) 바, 버, 보, 부, 브, 비
　(2) 다, 더, 도, 두, 드, 디
　(3) 사, 서, 소, 수, 스, 시
　(4) 자, 저, 조, 주, 즈, 지
　(5) 가, 거, 고, 구, 그, 기
　(6) 하, 허, 호, 후, 흐, 히

2 (1) 지구　　(2) 도시　　(3) 고기　　(4) 가수
(5) 두부　　(6) 그리고　(7) 보기　　(8) 아버지
(9) 하루　　(10) 서비스

3 비, 모자, 바지, 구두, 지도, 바다, 가수, 사자

STEP 5 **Quiz Yourself!**

1 (1) 조리　　(2) 바지　　(3) 거리　　(4) 주사
(5) 수다　　(6) 다리　　(7) 서기　　(8) 조수

2 (1) 거기　　(2) 소리　　(3) 지하　　(4) 기사
(5) 두부　　(6) 모기　　(7) 자리

Chapter 4

STEP 1 **Let's Warm Up!**

1 ⓐ밥　　　ⓑ국　　　ⓒ숟가락　ⓓ젓가락
ⓔ물　　　ⓕ김치　　ⓖ김　　　ⓗ찌개

2 (1) 물　　　(2) 밥　　　(3) 김　　　(4) 젓가락
(5) 국　　　(6) 김치

3 Ex. A: 뭐예요?　　B: 밥이에요.
(1) A: 뭐예요?　　B: 김치예요.
(2) A: 뭐예요?　　B: 젓가락이에요.
(3) A: 뭐예요?　　B: 물이에요.

STEP 2 **Let's Study!**

Listen (1) 밥　　(2) 물　　(3) 김　　　(4) 국

Practice (1) 아, 마　　　　(2) 아, 암

Practice
(1) 아, 암　(2) 아, 안　(3) 아, 알　(4) 아, 앙
(5) 아, 압　(6) 아, 악　(7) 아, 앝　(8) 아, 앗
(9) 아, 앛　(10) 아, 앟

*Pronunciation Point

1 (1) 삼, 산, 상　　　　(2) 감, 간, 강
(3) 밤, 반, 방　　　　(4) 담, 단, 당
(5) 잠, 잔, 장　　　　(6) 맘, 만, 망

2 (1) 맏, 맛, 맞, 맣　　(2) 낟, 낫, 낮, 낳

3 (1) 곡, 곤　(2) 목, 못　(3) 낙, 낮

4 (1) 좋아요 (2) 놓아요 (3) 넣어요

STEP 3 **Reading Activity!**

1 (1) 암, 엄, 옴, 움, 음, 임
(2) 간, 건, 곤, 군, 근, 긴
(3) 날, 널, 놀, 눌, 늘, 닐
(4) 상, 성, 송, 숭, 승, 싱
(5) 압, 업, 옵, 웁, 읍, 입
(6) 닥, 덕, 독, 둑, 득, 딕
(7) 앋, 얻, 옷, 옷, 읏, 잊
(8) 갇, 걷, 곳, 굿, 긎, 깋

2 (1) 강　　(2) 남　　(3) 돔　　(4) 만
(5) 굽　　(6) 빅　　(7) 낮　　(8) 짐
(9) 곳　　(10) 밤

3 (1) 곰　　(2) 근　　(3) 장　　(4) 성
(5) 목　　(6) 옷　　(7) 몸　　(8) 동
(9) 북

4 (1) 이름　　(2) 시간　　(3) 아들　　(4) 음식
(5) 수업　　(6) 아줌마　(7) 남산　　(8) 젓가락
(9) 도장　　(10) 거울　　(11) 한국　　(12) 밀가루

5 (1) 바람　　(2) 미국　　(3) 사진　　(4) 일곱
(5) 장소　　(6) 다섯

6 (1) 사진　　(2) 가방　　(3) 주말　　(4) 버섯

7 (1) 전문　　(2) 정말　　(3) 방문　　(4) 전기
(5) 성공　　(6) 선물

*Special Pronunciation Rule

Learn 음악, 종이

Practice

1 (1) 단어　　(2) 금일　　(3) 녹음　　(4) 만일
(5) 웃음　　(6) 믿음　　(7) 본인　　(8) 발음
(9) 언어　　(10) 직업　　(11) 길이　　(12) 얼음

2 (1) 발음　　(2) 웃음　　(3) 단어　　(4) 직업
(5) 음악　　(6) 얼음　　(7) 종이　　(8) 성인

STEP 4 **Writing Activity!**

1 (1) 밤, 반, 발, 방, 밥, 박
(2) 담, 단, 달, 당, 답, 닥
(3) 곤, 곳, 곶, 낟, 낮, 낳

2 (1) 기름　　(2) 시작　　(3) 부모님　(4) 이불
(5) 사랑　　(6) 아줌마

3 집, 문, 발, 목, 돈, 눈, 운동, 공항, 음식,
점심, 한복, 옷, 우산, 선물, 남자, 가방

STEP 5 Quiz Yourself!

1 (1) 섬   (2) 분   (3) 성   (4) 골

2 (1) 혼자   (2) 바람   (3) 장난   (4) 곧
    (5) 식당   (6) 명   (7) 동물   (8) 빚
    (9) 직업

3 (1) 김밥   (2) 만두   (3) 서울   (4) 부산

4 (1) 반   (2) 물   (3) 입   (4) 돈
    (5) 사랑   (6) 남자   (7) 실망   (8) 우선
    (9) 일본   (10) 가족   (11) 입구   (12) 못
    (13) 국

5 (1) 동   (2) 서   (3) 남   (4) 북

6 (1) 산   (2) 나무   (3) 강   (4) 절
    (5) 바다   (6) 섬   (7) 하늘   (8) 바람
    (9) 비   (10) 눈

Chapter 5

STEP 1 Let's Warm Up!

1 ⓐ테니스   ⓑ야구   ⓒ수영   ⓓ태권도
   ⓔ요가   ⓕ스키   ⓖ축구

2 (1) 수영   (2) 야구   (3) 태권도   (4) 요가
    (5) 축구

3 Ex.1 A: 테니스 잘해요?   B: 네, 잘해요.
   Ex.2 A: 축구 잘해요?   B: 아니요, 못해요.
   (1) A: 수영 잘해요?   B: 네, 잘해요.
   (2) A: 야구 잘해요?   B: 아니요, 못해요.
   (3) A: 요가 잘해요?   B: 아니요, 못해요.
   (4) A: 태권도 잘해요?   B: 네, 잘해요.

STEP 2 Let's Study!

Listen (1) 야구   (2) 요가   (3) 수영

Learn 야, 여, 요, 유

Practice

   (1) 아, 야   (2) 어, 여   (3) 오, 요   (4) 우, 유

*Pronunciation Point

1 요, 여

2 (1) 요리   (2) 여기   (3) 여가   (4) 영

Practice

1 (1) 야, 냐   (2) 여, 벼   (3) 요, 묘   (4) 유, 규
2 (1) 사, 샤   (2) 소, 쇼

STEP 3 Reading Activity!

1 (1) 야, 여, 요, 유   (2) 갸, 겨, 교, 규
    (3) 샤, 셔, 쇼, 슈   (4) 약, 역, 욕, 육

2 (1) 용   (2) 병   (3) 교   (4) 류
    (5) 향

3 (1) 역   (2) 연기   (3) 별   (4) 굴
    (5) 조용   (6) 요금   (7) 목욕   (8) 금연

4 (1) 서양   (2) 무료   (3) 기념   (4) 학교
    (5) 공연   (6) 현금   (7) 노력   (8) 경기
    (9) 연구

5 (1) 양말   (2) 안경   (3) 수요일   (4) 여유
    (5) 여자   (6) 주유소   (7) 중요   (8) 무역
    (9) 영어   (10) 여름   (11) 우유   (12) 일요일

6 (1) 야구   (2) 유리   (3) 수영   (4) 겨울
    (5) 무료   (6) 유명   (7) 연결   (8) 안녕

7 (1) 수염   (2) 저녁   (3) 양복   (4) 주유소

*Special Pronunciation Rule

Learn (1) 입문, 습니다   (2) 잇몸, 벚나무
       (3) 국민, 작년

Practice

1 (1) 작년   (2) 욕망   (3) 업무   (4) 숙모
    (5) 입니다   (6) 입문   (7) 빗물   (8) 식물
    (9) 잇몸   (10) 합니다   (11) 숙녀   (12) 잣나무

STEP 4 Writing Activity!

1 (1) 야, 여, 요, 유
    (2) 냐, 녀, 뇨, 뉴
    (3) 랴, 려, 료, 류

2 (1) 여기   (2) 조용   (3) 아니요   (4) 유리
    (5) 동양   (6) 며느리   (7) 연습   (8) 저녁
    (9) 영수증

3 약, 여자, 병, 우유, 요리, 영어, 안경, 유명

STEP 5 Quiz Yourself!

1 across ①수염   down ①수수료
   across ②여가   down ②여드름
   across ③여름   down ③여자

across ④서양인　　　down ④고양이
across ⑤안경　　　　down ⑤야경
across ⑥자유　　　　down ⑥안녕
across ⑦소유　　　　down ⑦주유소
across ⑧명동　　　　down ⑧유명

2 (1) 봄　　(2) 여름　　(3) 가을　　(4) 겨울

3 (1) 영어　(2) 용기　(3) 중요　(4) 수료
(5) 겨울　(6) 수영　(7) 면도　(8) 얼음
(9) 저녁

Chapter 6

STEP 1 Let's Warm Up!

1 ⓐ새우　ⓑ게　　ⓒ조개　ⓓ계란
ⓔ버섯　ⓕ호박

2 (1) 조개　(2) 새우　(3) 버섯　(4) 게
(5) 계란

3 Ex.1 A: 새우 좋아해요?　B: 네, 좋아해요.
Ex.2 A: 계란 좋아해요?　B: 아니요, 안좋아해요.
(1) A: 조개 좋아해요?　　B: 네, 좋아해요.
(2) A: 버섯 좋아해요?　　B: 아니요, 안좋아해요.
(3) A: 게 좋아해요?　　　B: 네, 좋아해요.
(4) A: 호박 좋아해요?　　B: 아니요, 안좋아해요.

STEP 2 Let's Study!

Listen (1) 새우　(2) 조개　(3) 게　(4) 계란

Learn 애, 에, 애, 예

Practice (1) 애, 얘　　　(2) 에, 예

*Pronunciation Point
(1) 개, 게　(2) 모래, 모레

STEP 3 Reading Activity!

1 (1) 애, 에, 얘, 예　　(2) 개, 게, 걔, 계
(3) 내, 네, 냬, 녜　　(4) 래, 레, 럐, 례

2 (1) 색　(2) 매　(3) 예　(4) 생
(5) 냇　(6) 해　(7) 겨　(8) 에

3 (1) 안내　(2) 아래　(3) 어제　(4) 예술
(5) 재미　(6) 시계　(7) 얘기　(8) 계단

4 (1) 예약　(2) 문제　(3) 남동생　(4) 계속
(5) 숙제　(6) 냉장고　(7) 내일　(8) 가게
(9) 얘기　(10) 인생　(11) 제주도　(12) 세상

5 (1) 시내　(2) 동대문　(3) 날개　(4) 면세점
(5) 실제　(6) 선생님　(7) 명예　(8) 무지개

6 (1) 배　(2) 생선　(3) 계단　(4) 시계

7 (1) 재미　(2) 생각　(3) 기대　(4) 소개
(5) 오래　(6) 예상　(7) 매일　(8) 계절
(9) 경제　(10) 생일　(11) 반대　(12) 세계

*Special Pronunciation Rule

Learn 신라, 설날

Practice

(1) 진리　(2) 연령　(3) 진료　(4) 실내
(5) 난리　(6) 논란　(7) 연락　(8) 신라
(9) 논리　(10) 설날　(11) 신랑　(12) 곤란

STEP 4 Writing Activity!

1 (1) 애, 얘, 에, 예
(2) 개, 걔, 게, 계
(3) 래, 럐, 레, 례

2 노래, 맥주, 계단, 베개, 냄새, 벌레, 비행기,
냉장고

STEP 5 Quiz Yourself!

1 시대, 배우, 언제, 기계, 인생, 예상, 세로,
생선, 아래, 계산

Chapter 7

STEP 1 Let's Warm Up!

1 ⓐ주스　ⓑ커피　ⓒ우유　ⓓ콜라
ⓔ아이스티　ⓕ녹차　ⓖ홍차
ⓗ사이다

2 (1) 녹차　(2) 콜라　(3) 커피　(4) 아이스티
(5) 우유

3 Ex. 커피 주세요.　　　(1) 콜라 주세요.
(2) 녹차 주세요.　　　(3) 아이스티 주세요.

STEP 2 Let's Study!

Listen (1) 콜라 (2) 커피 (3) 녹차 (4) 아이스티

Practice

(1) 바, 파 (2) 다, 타 (3) 자, 차 (4) 가, 카

*Pronunciation Point

(1) 발, 팔 (2) 동, 통 (3) 기자, 기차
(4) 그림, 크림

STEP 3 Reading Activity!

1 (1) 바, 파, 버, 퍼, 보, 포, 부, 푸, 브, 프, 비, 피
 (2) 다, 타, 더, 터, 도, 토, 두, 투, 드, 트, 디, 티
 (3) 자, 차, 저, 처, 조, 초, 주, 추, 즈, 츠, 지, 치
 (4) 가, 카, 거, 커, 고, 코, 구, 쿠, 그, 크, 기, 키

2 (1) 팔　　 (2) 덕　　 (3) 춤　　 (4) 공
 (5) 피　　 (6) 탕　　 (7) 키　　 (8) 팀
 (9) 층　　 (10) 포

3 (1) 포도　 (2) 차요　 (3) 동기　 (4) 판사
 (5) 다기　 (6) 처음　 (7) 처리　 (8) 그림

4 (1) 크기　 (2) 봉투　 (3) 자동차 (4) 김치
 (5) 스포츠 (6) 경치　 (7) 선택　 (8) 추석
 (9) 지하철 (10) 통역　 (11) 출구　 (12) 부탁

5 (1) 부터　 (2) 카메라 (3) 파도　 (4) 토요일
 (5) 우표　 (6) 우체국 (7) 친절　 (8) 통조림

6 (1) 아침　 (2) 코　　 (3) 표　　 (4) 경찰

*Special Pronunciation Rule

Learn (1) 급히, 축하　 (2) 좋다, 넣고

Practice

1 (1) 좋고　 (2) 입학　 (3) 못해요 (4) 이렇게
 (5) 놓다　 (6) 맏형　 (7) 육 호선 (8) 그렇지

2 (1) 연습해요　　　 (2) 생각해요
 (3) 행복해요　　　 (4) 비슷해요

STEP 4 Writing Activity!

1 (1) 파, 퍼, 포, 푸, 프, 피
 (2) 타, 터, 토, 투, 트, 티
 (3) 차, 처, 초, 추, 츠, 치
 (4) 카, 커, 코, 쿠, 크, 키

2 (1) 포도　 (2) 보통　 (3) 김치　 (4) 남편
 (5) 출발　 (6) 도착　 (7) 연필　 (8) 갈비탕
 (9) 친구　 (10) 컴퓨터

3 자동차, 주차장, 지하철, 택시, 기차,
 선풍기, 자판기, 세탁기, 코, 표, 책,
 친구, 아침, 핸드폰, 침대, 단추

STEP 5 Quiz Yourself!

1 (1) 콩　　 (2) 불　　 (3) 추석　 (4) 컵
 (5) 턱　　 (6) 짐　　 (7) 조상　 (8) 털
 (9) 자판　 (10) 저장　 (11) 포기　 (12) 편해요

2 (1) 일　　 (2) 이　　 (3) 삼　　 (4) 사
 (5) 오　　 (6) 육　　 (7) 칠　　 (8) 팔
 (9) 구　　 (10) 십　　 (11) 영, 공

3 (1) 택시　 (2) 추억　 (3) 평일　 (4) 삼촌
 (5) 스키　 (6) 처음　 (7) 배추　 (8) 풀
 (9) 교통　 (10) 사촌　 (11) 칭찬　 (12) 청소
 (13) 피부　 (14) 만큼　 (15) 에어컨 (16) 카메라
 (17) 핸드폰　　　　 (18) 커피
 (19) 녹차　　　　　 (20) 표
 (21) 책　　　　　　 (22) 경찰
 (23) 통역　　　　　 (24) 칠판

4 (1) 한국　 (2) 미국　 (3) 중국　 (4) 영국
 (5) 일본　 (6) 호주　 (7) 독일　 (8) 인도
 (9) 캐나다 (10) 프랑스 (11) 필리핀 (12) 베트남

5 (1) 명동　 (2) 남산　 (3) 시청　 (4) 홍대
 (5) 남대문 시장　　　 (6) 동대문 시장
 (7) 경복궁　　　　　 (8) 광화문
 (9) 강남역　　　　　 (10) 서울역
 (11) 이태원　　　　　 (12) 종로

Chapter **8**

STEP 1 Let's Warm Up!

1 ⓐ돈　　 ⓑ지도　 ⓒ지갑　 ⓓ열쇠
 ⓔ여권　 ⓕ우산　 ⓖ책　　 ⓗ휴지
 ⓘ핸드폰 ⓙ외국인 등록증

2 (1) 지갑　 (2) 여권　 (3) 돈　　 (4) 열쇠
 (5) 책　　 (6) 외국인 등록증

3 Ex1. A: 핸드폰 있어요?　　 B: 네, 있어요.
 Ex2. A: 핸드폰 있어요?　　 B: 아니요, 없어요.
 (1) A: 지갑 있어요?　　　 B: 네, 있어요.
 (2) A: 여권 있어요?　　　 B: 아니요, 없어요.
 (3) A: 열쇠 있어요?　　　 B: 아니요, 없어요.

(4) A: 외국인 등록증 있어요?
　　B: 네, 있어요.

STEP 2 Let's Study!

Listen (1) 외국인 등록증　(2) 열쇠　(3) 여권

Learn 와, 워, 왜, 웨, 외, 위, 의

Practice

(1) 오, 아, 와　　　　(2) 우, 어, 워
(3) 오, 애, 왜　　　　(4) 우, 에, 웨
(5) 오, 이, 외　　　　(6) 우, 이, 위
(7) 으, 이, 의

*Pronunciation Point

1 왜, 웨, 외

2 (1) ⓐ왜　　ⓑ위기　　ⓒ외국
　　(2) ⓐ열쇠　ⓑ인쇄　　ⓒ부숴요
　　(3) ⓐ전화　ⓑ사회　　ⓒ훼손
　　(4) ⓐ괴물　ⓑ일궈요　ⓒ궤도

STEP 3 Reading Activity!

1 (1) 와, 워, 왜, 웨, 외, 위, 의
　　(2) 과, 궈, 괘, 궤, 괴, 귀, 긔
　　(3) 화, 훠, 홰, 훼, 회, 휘, 희

2 (1) 왜　　(2) 와　　(3) 괴　　(4) 회
　　(5) 되　　(6) 귀　　(7) 니　　(8) 의
　　(9) 쥐　　(10) 원

3 (1) 쇠　　(2) 사회　(3) 해　　(4) 의사
　　(5) 뒤　　(6) 주위　(7) 뭐　　(8) 인쇄
　　(9) 죄　　(10) 외국

4 (1) 과일　　(2) 추워요　(3) 의견　　(4) 위험
　　(5) 영화　　(6) 매워요　(7) 병원　　(8) 교회
　　(9) 희망　　(10) 대사관 (11) 취소　　(12) 최고

5 (1) 사과　　(2) 화장실　(3) 회사　　(4) 더워요
　　(5) 의사　　(6) 좌회전　(7) 돼지　　(8) 외국인
　　(9) 훼손　　(10) 휘파람

6 (1) 가위　　(2) 의자　　(3) 영화　　(4) 만 원

*Special Pronunciation Rule

Learn (1) 의자, 주의　(2) 희망, 무늬

Practice

(1) 예의　　(2) 논의　　(3) 편의점　(4) 의문
(5) 저희　　(6) 흰색　　(7) 의미　　(8) 여의도

(9) 무늬　　(10) 회의　　(11) 한의원　(12) 너희
(13) 의사　(14) 거의　　(15) 의자

STEP 4 Writing Activity!

1 (1) 와, 위, 애, 웨, 이, 위, 이
　　(2) 과, 귀, 괘, 궤, 괴, 귀, 긔
　　(3) 화, 훠, 홰, 훼, 회, 휘, 희

2 (1) 영화　　(2) 의자　　(3) 외교　　(4) 주위
　　(5) 돼지　　(6) 죄송　　(7) 희망　　(8) 외국
　　(9) 관심　　(10)영원　　(11) 분위기 (12) 쉬워요

3 (1) ⓐ결과 ⓑ과자　　(2) ⓐ추위 ⓑ위험
　　(3) ⓐ의심 ⓑ의미　　(4) ⓐ취미 ⓑ취소
　　(5) ⓐ문화 ⓑ전화　　(6) ⓐ쉬워 ⓑ매워

4 과일, 전화, 쥐, 돼지, 바위, 바퀴, 영화, 주의

STEP 5 Quiz Yourself!

1 (1) 월요일 (2) 화요일 (3) 수요일 (4) 목요일
　　(5) 금요일 (6) 토요일 (7) 일요일

2 (1) 호박　　(2) 파　　(3) 오이　　(4) 양파
　　(5) 고추　　(6) 마늘　　(7) 당근　　(8) 감자
　　(9) 고구마

3 은행, 편의점, 병원, 영화관, 공항, 집,
　　주차장, 화장실

4 (1) 선생님 (2) 학생　　(3) 경찰　　(4) 회사원
　　(5) 주부　　(6) 가수　　(7) 의사　　(8) 간호사
　　(9) 기자　　(10) 화가

Chapter 9

STEP 1 Let's Warm Up!

1 ⓐ아빠　　ⓑ엄마　　ⓒ오빠　　ⓓ언니
　　ⓔ아들　　ⓕ딸

2 (1) 오빠　　(2) 언니　　(3) 엄마　　(4) 아빠
　　(5) 딸

3 Ex. A: 누구예요?　　B: 엄마예요.
　　(1) A: 누구예요?　　B: 아빠예요.
　　(2) A: 누구예요?　　B: 오빠예요.
　　(3) A: 누구예요?　　B: 딸이에요.

STEP 2 Let's Study!

Listen (1) 아빠　　(2) 오빠　　(3) 딸

Practice

(1) 바, 빠　(2) 다, 따　(3) 사, 싸
(4) 자, 짜　(5) 가, 까

*Pronunciation Point

(1) 불, 풀, 뿔　　　　(2) 달, 탈, 딸
(3) 자요, 차요, 짜요　(4) 굴, 쿨, 꿀
(5) 살, 쌀

STEP 3 Reading Activity!

1 (1) 바, 빠, 버, 뻐, 보, 뽀, 부, 뿌, 브, 쁘, 비, 삐
　(2) 다, 따, 더, 떠, 도, 또, 두, 뚜, 드, 뜨, 디, 띠
　(3) 사, 싸, 서, 써, 소, 쏘, 수, 쑤, 스, 쓰, 시, 씨
　(4) 자, 짜, 저, 쩌, 조, 쪼, 주, 쭈, 즈, 쯔, 지, 찌
　(5) 가, 까, 거, 꺼, 고, 꼬, 구, 꾸, 그, 끄, 기, 끼

2 (1) 딸　　(2) 짐　　(3) 꼭　　(4) 분
　(5) 시　　(6) 뜻　　(7) 꿈　　(8) 죽
　(9) 쌀　　(10) 뺨

3 (1) 방　　(2) 때문　(3) 쌈　　(4) 가지
　(5) 곡　　(6) 싸요　(7) 뼈　　(8) 자리

4 (1) 토끼　　(2) 빵　　(3) 가끔　　(4) 깨끗이
　(5) 눈썹　　(6) 떡　　(7) 어쩐지　(8) 뿌리
　(9) 아저씨　(10) 짝　　(11) 뚜껑　　(12) 씨름

5 (1) 공짜　　(2) 이따가　(3) 빨리　　(4) 코끼리
　(5) 느낌　　(6) 오른쪽　(7) 찌개　　(8) 바빠요
　(9) 싸움　　(10) 가까워

6 (1) 어깨　　(2) 딸기　　(3) 빵　　(4) 찌개

*Special Pronunciation Rule

Learn 입구, 곧장, 식당, 역시

Practice

1 (1) 혹시　(2) 옷장　　(3) 갑자기　(4) 덕분
　(5) 목적　(6) 목소리　(7) 집중　　(8) 역시
　(9) 각각　(10) 늦게　　(11) 습관　　(12) 숟가락

2 (1) 약속　(2) 책상　　(3) 듣기　　(4) 입구
　(5) 박수　(6) 낮잠

STEP 4 Writing Activity!

1 (1) 빠, 뻐, 뽀, 뿌, 쁘, 삐
　(2) 따, 떠, 또, 뚜, 뜨, 띠

(3) 싸, 써, 쏘, 쑤, 쓰, 씨
(4) 짜, 쩌, 쪼, 쭈, 쯔, 찌
(5) 까, 꺼, 꼬, 꾸, 끄, 끼

2 (1) 자꾸　(2) 솜씨　　(3) 빨래　(4) 가짜
　(5) 잠깐　(6) 비싸요　(7) 깜짝　(8) 아저씨
　(9) 말씀　(10) 기뻐요

3 꿈, 꼬리, 땀, 뚜껑, 쓰레기통, 짜요,
　찜질방, 오빠, 쌍둥이, 오른쪽, 빵,
　어깨, 토끼, 비싸요, 떡, 공짜

STEP 5 Quiz Yourself!

1 (1) 떡　　(2) 죽　　(3) 키　　(4) 분
　(5) 씨름　(6) 참　　(7) 또　　(8) 져요
　(9) 깨요

2 (1) 쓰기　(2) 쯤　　(3) 진짜　(4) 글쎄
　(5) 살짝　(6) 일찍　(7) 함께　(8) 또
　(9) 벌써　(10) 나빠요　(11) 그때　(12) 따로
　(13) 싸움　(14) 똑바로　(15) 짜증　(16) 꾸중
　(17) 빵집　(18) 짜리　(19) 뿌리　(20) 꼭지
　(21) 쑥　(22) 손뼉　(23) 깜짝　(24) 예뻐요
　(25) 팔꿈치

3 (1) 사과　(2) 배　　(3) 딸기　(4) 포도
　(5) 수박　(6) 바나나　(7) 감　　(8) 귤

Chapter 10

STEP 1 Let's Warm Up!

1 (1) 하나　(2) 둘　　(3) 셋　　(4) 넷
　(5) 다섯　(6) 여섯　(7) 일곱　(8) 여덟
　(9) 아홉　(10) 열

2 (1) 세 개　(2) 아홉 개　(3) 여섯 개　(4) 두 개

STEP 2 Let's Study!

Final Consonants ㅍ, ㅌ, ㅊ, ㅋ, ㅆ, ㄲ

Listen (1) 잎　(2) 끝　(3) 낮　(4) 밖

Practice (1) 아, 파　　(2) 아, 앞

Practice

(1) 아, 앞, 압　　　(2) 아, 악, 앜
(3) 아, 앆, 악　　　(4) 나, 낱, 낟
(5) 나, 낮, 낯, 낫, 낟　(6) 나, 났, 낟

*Pronunciation Point

(1) 입, 잎　(2) 박, 밖　(3) 빗, 빚, 빛

Double Final Consonants

Listen (1) 갑　(2) 목　(3) 닥　(4) 삼

Learn (1) 앉다, 많고, 여덟, 핥다, 옳지,
　　　 없다, 삯
　　 (2) 흙, 까닭, 앎, 삶

STEP 3 Reading Activity!

1 (1) 앞, 옆, 짚, 숲　(2) 끝, 팥, 낱, 홑
　 (3) 밑, 빛, 꽃, 숯　(4) 억, 녘
　 (5) 었, 갔, 섰, 했　(6) 밖, 닦, 낚, 솎
　 (7) 몫, 삯　(8) 값, 없
　 (9) 닭, 칡　(10) 앎, 삶

2 (1) 솥　(2) 육　(3) 밖　(4) 흘
　 (5) 값　(6) 꽃　(7) 역　(8) 삶
　 (9) 밑　(10) 멱

3 (1) ⓐ꼭 ⓑ꽃 ⓒ꽃　(2) ⓐ숨 ⓑ숨 ⓒ숲
　 (3) ⓐ낙 ⓑ낚 ⓒ났　(4) ⓐ숯 ⓑ숫 ⓒ숙

4 (1) 겉　(2) 갔다　(3) 몇　(4) 낚아요
　 (5) 닭　(6) 했어요　(7) 몫　(8) 앉아요

5 (1) 여덟　(2) 돌솥　(3) 갔어요　(4) 바깥
　 (5) 눈빛　(6) 까닭　(7) 닭고기　(8) 무릎
　 (9) 부엌　(10) 꽃병　(11) 숯불　(12) 있어요

6 (1) 돌솥　(2) 잎　(3) 빛　(4) 흙

*Special Pronunciation Rule

Learn

1 (1) 앞, 앞이　(2) 밖, 밖에
　 (3) 꽃, 꽃이　(4) 빛, 빛을

2 (1) 닭, 닭이　(2) 값, 값을
　 (3) 삶, 삶에　(4) 삯, 삯을

3 (1) 많이　(2) 않아요　(3) 싫어요　(4) 잃어요

Practice

(1) 많이　(2) 끝에　(3) 무릎에　(4) 밑줄
(5) 꽃을　(6) 싫어요　(7) 읽은　(8) 몇살
(9) 젊음　(10) 옆집　(11) 볶음　(12) 없어요

STEP 4 Writing Activity!

1 (1) 앞, 숲, 짚, 끝, 밭, 팥
　 (2) 꽃, 낯, 빛, 엌, 밖, 있
　 (3) 닭, 삶, 값, 몫, 앉, 않

2 끝, 숲, 무릎, 꽃, 부엌, 밖, 닭, 값

STEP 5 Quiz Yourself!

1 (1) ⓐ마이　ⓑ마니　ⓒ많이
　 (2) ⓐ안자서　ⓑ앉아서　ⓒ안아서
　 (3) ⓐ일어요　ⓑ일러요　ⓒ잃어요
　 (4) ⓐ다가요　ⓑ다까요　ⓒ닦아요

2 (1) 바깥　(2) 진흙
　 (3) 잎　(4) 숱
　 (5) 값이　(6) 몇 시
　 (7) 꽃이　(8) 부엌
　 (9) 콩팥　(10) 굶어요
　 (11) 낚시　(12) 핥아요
　 (13) 짧아요　(14) 많아요
　 (15) 읽어요　(16) 긁어요
　 (17) 젊어요　(18) 앉아서
　 (19) 숲　(20) 옆
　 (21) 많고　(22) 앓다
　 (23) 찜닭　(24) 떡볶이

3 잎이, 밟아요, 낡아요, 잃어버렸어요,
　 많아요, 몇 번, 없어요, 갔어요, 않아요

4 (1) 앞　(2) 뒤　(3) 옆　(4) 오른쪽
　 (5) 왼쪽　(6) 위　(7) 밑　(8) 안
　 (9) 밖

5 (1) 머리　(2) 눈　(3) 코　(4) 가슴
　 (5) 배　(6) 귀　(7) 입　(8) 목
　 (9) 어깨　(10) 허리　(11) 무릎　(12) 발
　 (13) 팔　(14) 손　(15) 다리

Index

ㄴ

01
ⓐ 안녕하세요?
ⓑ 안녕하세요?
track 222

02
안녕히 가세요.
track 223

03
안녕히 계세요.
track 224

04
ⓐ 감사합니다.
ⓑ 네.
track 225

05
ⓐ 미안합니다.
ⓑ 괜찮아요.
track 226

06
실례합니다.
track 227

02

Goodbye.

(Said to the person who is leaving.)

01

ⓐ Hello?
ⓑ Hello?

04

ⓐ Thank you.
ⓑ You're welcome.

03

Goodbye.

(Said to the person who is staying.)

06

Excuse me.

05

ⓐ I'm sorry.
ⓑ That's okay.

07

얼마예요?

track 228

08

다른 건 없어요?

track 229

09

너무 비싸요.

track 230

10

좀 깎아 주세요.

track 231

11

화장실이
어디에 있어요?

track 232

12

(경복궁)에
어떻게 가요?

track 233

08

Do you have
anything different?

07

How much is it?

10

Please give me
a discount.

09

It's too expensive.

12

How can I get to
(Gyeongbokgung
Palace)?

11

Where is
the bathroom?

13 이게 뭐예요?

track 234

14 알겠어요.

track 235

15 잘 모르겠어요.

track 236

16 맛있어요.

track 237

17 너무 매워요.

track 238

18 아니요, 괜찮아요.

track 239

14

I see.
I understand.

13

What is this?

16

It's delicious.

15

I don't know.

18

No, thank you.

17

It's too spicy.

19
여보세요.

track 240

20
잠깐만요.

track 241

21
아파요.

track 242

22
다시 한번
말해 주세요.

track 243

23
한국어 잘 못해요.

track 244

24
도와주세요.

track 245

20

Just a moment,
please.

19

Hello.
(on the phone)

22

Please say that
one more time.

21

I'm sick.
It hurts.

24

Please help me.

23

I can't speak
Korean well.